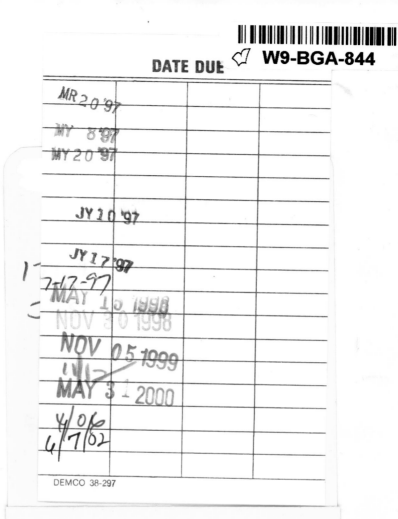

Euthanasia

The "Right to Die" Issue

Daniel Jussim

—Issues in Focus—

ENSLOW PUBLISHERS, INC.

Bloy St. and Ramsey Ave.   P. O. Box 38
Box 777   Aldershot
Hillside, N.J. 07205   Hants GU12 6BP
U.S.A.   U.K.

Library of Congress Cataloging-in-Publication Data

Jussim, Daniel.
     Euthanasia / Jussim, Daniel.
       p. cm.
     'Includes bibliographical references and index.
     Summary: Discusses passive and active euthanasia and some ethical
and moral issues surrounding the topic.
     ISBN 0-89490-429-9
     1. Euthanasia—Juvenile literature. [1. Euthanasia.] I. Title.
R726.J87 1993
179'.7—dc20
                                        92-42147
                                          CIP
                                          AC

Printed in the United States of America

10 9 8 7 6 5 4 3 2 1

Illustration Credits:
Copyright Choice In Dying, Inc. Reprinted by permission, pp. 32, 37;
Courtesy of Betty Rollin, p. 61; Courtesy of Joyce Cruzan, p. 23; Courtesy
of Ralph Mero, pp. 94, 97; Photo by Billings, p. 70.

Cover Illustration: Courtesy of Jules Rose

The Advance Directive reproduced on pages 34–35 is reprinted by
permission of Choice in Dying, Inc. (formerly Concern for Dying/Society
for the Right to Die), 200 Varick Street, New York, N.Y. 10014,
212-366-5540.

Acknowledgments

My thanks to the following people for their help: to Bruce Jennings, who reviewed the manuscript; and to Kathi Hamlon of the International Anti-Euthanasia Task Force; Joel Roselin of Choice in Dying, Inc.; Diana Smith of the Hemlock Society; and Dana Points; all of whom provided valuable material. My thanks also to Walter Billings, Rev. Ralph Mero, Betty Rollin, and Christy Cruzan White, who provided photographs.

Contents

Part I: Passive Euthanasia

1 "Killing" or "Letting Die"? 7

2 The Dilemma of
    Unconscious Patients 14

3 Some Other Dilemmas 39

**Part II: Active Euthanasia and
Assisted Suicide**

4 The Lethal Dose 50

5 Aiding the Death of a
    Loved One 60

6 When Doctors Aid in Suicide 75

7 Should Active Euthanasia
    Be Legalized? 87

Chapter Notes 101

For Further Information 108

Index 109

I

Passive
Euthanasia

1

"Killing" or "Letting Die"?

When you become ill, most likely you do whatever your doctor says you need to do to get better. You take medicine that may taste bad or get an injection that hurts a little. You may not enjoy this, but you know it's the right thing to do because it will make you well again.

But sometimes people become so ill that their condition is hopeless. Medicine may extend their lives for a time, but they will never recover, and their sickness will soon end in their death. This condition is called a "terminal illness." A person can also fall into an unconscious state due to illness or injury. He may live many years in this state, even though there is no hope he will ever regain consciousness.

Medical technology has made fantastic advances in

the twentieth century. It has given us antibiotics to fight infections, vaccines that prevent illness, machines that help people breathe, and the ability to transplant bodily organs. But the large number of terminally ill and permanently unconscious patients alive today reflects an irony of modern medicine: Although it sometimes works wonders in curing people with serious illnesses, in many cases medicine cannot do this. Instead, medicine may be able only to preserve patients in a diminished condition while they wait to die.

Hopelessly ill patients may be in unrelievable physical pain, or their dependent condition may make them feel degraded and helpless. Because of this they may not want their life prolonged by all the machinery available to doctors today. In fact, they may believe that it is actually their *death* that is being prolonged. They may ask for life-support equipment to be disconnected so they can die peacefully, quickly, and with dignity. This is known as "passive voluntary euthanasia." (The term *euthanasia* is derived from a Greek word meaning "easy death.")

Doctors are trained to do everything possible to preserve life. All their professional instincts tell them to try to defeat death, or at least delay it for as long as possible. Medical personnel will always use "ordinary care" to help a patient, no matter how bad his condition. For instance, they will change a weak and terminally ill patient's position from time to time so he won't develop bedsores.

But most doctors will not use clearly "extraordinary" means (unusual, aggressive, or intrusive treatments) to save hopelessly ill patients who would prefer to die. For example, a patient may have advanced cancer and be in great pain. If his heart stops suddenly, doctors aren't likely to try to revive him if he has given them advance instructions to this effect. In many cases reviving him would be considered a cruel use of an aggressive treatment in a hopeless situation. Doctors would say that by not reviving him they are not killing him but rather *letting the patient die.*

A more ambiguous situation occurs when a patient wants life-support equipment, such as a respirator (a mechanical device that pumps air into and out of the lungs), disconnected so that he can die. Many doctors believe that disconnecting respirators in certain circumstances is acceptable. They say that a respirator is an extraordinary means of treatment because it is an intrusive device introduced by modern technology.

They also feel that disconnecting a respirator can be considered *letting die* rather than killing: The patient has an illness that prevents him from breathing naturally, and when the machine is turned off, it is the illness that kills him. Usually these doctors arrive at an understanding privately with a patient or his family, sometimes after also consulting a hospital ethics committee, and the respirator is turned off.

Other doctors say that a respirator is not "extraordinary"

because its use has become routine in modern medical care. They see it as one of many tools available to maintain patients. They also argue that because the doctors who disconnect respirators know that the patient will die, they therefore are taking a direct, deliberate action that produces death.

In the view of some doctors, then, "pulling the plug" is morally or legally equivalent to *killing* the patient, not merely letting him die, and is thus a form of murder. These doctors would find such an action unacceptable and would refuse a patient's request to turn off the respirator, thus setting the stage for a legal confrontation between physician and patient. One of the most private decisions a person can make may then become a subject of news stories and public controversy.

Whose Life Is It, Anyway?

People who side with the patient's request in this scenario are said to advocate his "right to die." They ask, "Whose life is it, anyway?" and answer that it is the patient's life, and therefore he should be allowed to make important decisions about it, even if some other people would disagree with those decisions.

They believe that patients who have a poor "quality of life" should be allowed to choose for themselves whether medical technology is to be used to prolong their lives. They point to certain individual rights that are protected by the U.S. Constitution or by state law,

10

such as the right to privacy or liberty, which, they feel, mean citizens can refuse medical care. V ρ 9.

2 In addition, right-to-die advocates point out that it can be very expensive to maintain people on life support, and the cost is often borne by the government. Allowing people to choose to end treatment is one way to fight the nation's soaring health care bills.

People who oppose the right-to-die concept are said to believe in the "sanctity of life." They argue that all human beings, no matter what their quality of life, have intrinsic worth and dignity. Therefore, they say, no one should be denied treatment by having life support withdrawn.

Sanctity-of-life advocates note that no one's life is totally his own, that individuals belong to the human community. To preserve this community, they say, the state should preserve human life—and the state's interest in doing this is more important than anyone's individual rights. This means the state should side with doctors who want to continue treatment against a patient who wants treatment withdrawn.

Some people also fear that a "right to die" for some will become a "duty to die" for others: Pressure to control health care costs could result in disabled people being deprived of care against their will. People favoring the sanctity-of-life concept point out, too, that doctors sometimes make mistakes. It is possible that some patients who die after refusing treatment would have unexpectedly recovered had they been kept alive.

Other factors complicate the argument. In cases where the patient is unconscious or too sick to communicate, his wishes concerning use of life-support equipment are not known unless he stated them ahead of time. The patient's family may try to make a decision for him, claiming that since they are the closest people to him they are in the best position to say what he would have wanted. Others believe that a family's complex emotional ties to the patient, and possible self-interest, would prevent them from making an objective decision.

The complex debate over the right to die has been raging in the press, the courts, in legislatures, and in religious institutions since the 1970s. It has been joined by religious leaders, lawyers, politicians, and moral philosophers called "medical ethicists." Some groups that advocate the right to die include Choice in Dying, the American Civil Liberties Union, and the American Medical Association. Opposing them are organizations that also oppose abortion, like the National Right to Life Committee, as well as the International Anti-Euthanasia Task Force and groups for disabled people, such as the Association for Retarded Citizens. In 1989 these forces squared off in the first right-to-die controversy to reach the U.S. Supreme Court.

The word *euthanasia* is defined in one dictionary as "the act of killing or permitting the death of hopelessly sick or injured individuals in a relatively painless way for reasons of mercy." Part I of this book looks at several dramatic true-life cases involving passive voluntary euthanasia—the withdrawal of treatment, upon a patient's request, to let him die. These will help you understand the issue and how it touches people's lives, and also let you come to your own conclusions about whether or not the practice of passive euthanasia should be permitted.

Passive voluntary euthanasia is distinguished from "active voluntary euthanasia" and "assisted suicide," practices that are even more controversial. In active voluntary euthanasia, a doctor gives a hopelessly ill patient, at the patient's request, an injection of deadly drugs. In assisted suicide, a patient is given a prescription for a lethal dose of pills. These practices will be discussed in Part II.

2

The Dilemma of Unconscious Patients

The Case of Karen Ann Quinlan: The Right to Die Makes Headlines

On April 14, 1975, Karen Ann Quinlan,[1] a twenty-one-year-old from a small town in New Jersey, passed out at a party after drinking gin and tonics and consuming a small quantity of tranquilizers. For a time she stopped breathing. Friends attempted mouth-to-mouth resuscitation and then took her, still unconscious, to the nearest hospital. She was later brought to St. Clare's Hospital in Denville, New Jersey.

For a while Karen's family had hope that she might recover. Karen was the daughter of Joseph and Julia Quinlan, an Irish Catholic couple who had adopted her and later had two children of their own. As Julia sat at Karen's bedside, she squeezed Karen's hand and thought she felt her squeeze back, but Julia knew she might have just imagined that.

Because the brain needs a constant flow of oxygen, Karen had sustained severe brain damage when she had stopped breathing. Doctors eventually diagnosed her as being in a "persistent vegetative state" (PVS), a condition of permanent unconsciousness (see page 16). She was never to squeeze another's hand again.

Before she lost consciousness, Karen was athletic and liked the outdoors; she loved to read and played the piano and sang. Her parents described her as friendly and outgoing. Though her teachers said she could have been an excellent student, she received mediocre grades in high school because she found it confining. High school friends said she was quiet but popular with boys. According to a former employer, she was a good, hard worker. Karen had moved out of her parents' house only a few months before she was hospitalized.

About a year after Karen lost consciousness, journalist Phyllis Battelle visited her in the hospital. The young woman who had been so active was now immobilized; she received food through tubes inserted in her nostrils, antibiotics through a tube connected to her kidneys, and air through a respirator, which pumped oxygen through

What Is PVS?

Patients in a persistent vegetative state have no self-aware-ness nor any awareness of their surroundings because the thinking part of the brain, the cerebral cortex, is dead. They cannot hear, see, feel, or smell. However, they can open their eyes, and they go through sleep-awake cycles. The more primitive part of the brain, the brain stem, still works, regulating breathing, blood pressure, and heart rate; and the body's other organs remain functional.

Because of these things, the condition is not considered "brain death," the legal and medical definition of death in the United States. In brain death, brain tissue breaks down; the whole brain stops working; lungs and heart function only with help from machines; and bodily organs soon deteriorate. Some countries define death differently. In Japan, for in-stance, a person is not considered dead unless his heart has stopped beating. PVS patients may live indefinitely; the longest reported survival of a person in PVS was 37 years, 111 days. Each year in the United States 5,000 to 10,000 people enter persistent vegetative states.

Although there has been at least one case in which a patient thought to be in PVS regained consciousness (the diagnosis had been wrong), when someone is actually in PVS this is impossible—she will be unconscious until she dies. Bioethicist Bruce Jennings argues that when tests are done properly, the PVS diagnosis, accomplished by sophisti-cated brain scans, is as accurate as any in medicine.[2]

a hole made in her throat. Battelle described Karen's appearance this way:

> The hands were drawn tight over the chest, the wrists sharply cocked so that the long, white fingers pointed straight downward, stiff and thin as pencils. . . . The eyes, still intensely blue, roved wildly, never quite focusing, and her mouth closed and opened in a series of grimaces. . . . Her knees were pulled up taut against her chest, her legs twisted and entangled.[3]

Given her pathetic condition, Karen's parents began to think it would be better to disconnect their daughter's respirator and let nature take its course. Joseph consulted the family's priest, Father Thomas Trapasso. Fr. Trapasso told Joseph Quinlan that the Roman Catholic Church had historically allowed extraordinary medical care to be ended in cases where a patient's condition was hopeless. But Joseph wasn't so sure. If he asked doctors to disconnect the respirator so Karen could die, would that be "playing God?" he asked. No, the priest answered, it would just be going along with a decision God had already made.

The Quinlans did make the decision to have the respirator disconnected, but to their surprise doctors at the hospital refused to comply when asked to do so. One said he had a "moral problem" with doing so. This refusal was to turn the Quinlans' private dilemma into the first celebrated right-to-die court case, one that would set an important legal precedent and expand public awareness of the issue.

Joseph Quinlan brought the case, which now made newspaper headlines, to a New Jersey superior court. He asked the court to authorize disconnection of the respirator so Karen could die "with grace and dignity." He testified about his religious feelings, saying that he wanted to "place her completely in the hands of the Lord and let His will be done."

Religious groups in the United States generally condemn active euthanasia, but they are each divided about the withdrawal of care from hopelessly ill patients. It is a matter of especially intense debate within the Catholic Church. While Father Trapasso and New Jersey's four Catholic bishops supported Karen Quinlan's right to die, others disagreed. A Vatican commentator wrote: "A right to death does not exist. . . . Love for life, even a life reduced to a 'ruin,' drives one to protect life with every possible care."

Joseph Quinlan's attorney argued that guarantees of privacy in the United States Constitution gave Karen the right to have her life support disconnected. As evidence that this is what Karen would have wanted, a longtime friend of Karen's testified that she had discussed with her the cancer of the mother of a mutual acquaintance. "Karen stated that if it was her, she would not want to be kept alive by machines under any circumstances," the friend said. Julia Quinlan testified to the same thing and added, "She wanted to enjoy life. And that's why when I see her in this condition, I know in my heart as her mother it is not what Karen would want to be."

Karen's temporary court-appointed representative, however, argued that she had a constitutional "right to life." The hospital's lawyer said the court should leave the decision to Karen's doctors, who were best qualified to make treatment decisions. And the attorney for her doctor declared that if the court sided with Karen's parents, then "hundreds of thousands of people who are confined to institutions for the chronically ill" would be in jeopardy because they "may be in a condition similar to Karen's and you can terminate their lives."

Judge Robert Muir, Jr., ruled that removing the respirator "would be homicide and an act of euthanasia" and said that "judicial conscience and morality" told him that Karen's physician was dealing with the case correctly. Even though Karen was "on the threshold of death," under the law no "humanitarian motives" can justify taking life. He also made these points: (1) Even if Karen had expressed a wish not to have her life prolonged by artificial means, she had done so when healthy and not "under solemn and sobering fact that death was a distinct choice." (2) A patient expects a doctor to "do all within his human power to favor life against death." (3) While Joseph Quinlan was a "very sincere, moral, ethical, and religious person," he was not the best person to make decisions for his daughter. He might be influenced by "his anguish."

The New Jersey Supreme Court's Decision in *Quinlan*

When Karen's parents appealed to the Supreme Court of New Jersey, however, Judge Muir's decision was reversed in a landmark ruling handed down on March 31, 1976. Seven judges unanimously held that Karen had a constitutional right of privacy to refuse treatment, and that this right could be exercised by her parents in her behalf. The court ruled that the right to refuse medical treatment increased as the "degree of bodily invasion increases and the prognosis dims." Because a respirator is invasive (it forces air into and out of the lungs) and Karen's unconsciousness was permanent, the court allowed the respirator to be withdrawn.

After the decision Karen's mother said, "I can't use the word glad or happy, because we're going to lose our daughter, but I'm thankful." She said she felt that God had preserved her daughter's life to help others by creating a legal precedent on the withdrawal of care. Karen was moved to a nursing home and removed from the respirator. Contrary to expectations, she did not die then, but started breathing on her own. She survived in her unconscious state for another ten years, sustained by tube-feeding.

Since the Quinlan controversy, most state courts that have handled right-to-die cases have allowed medical treatment to be withdrawn from hopelessly ill patients—

including unconscious ones whose family requested this. A recent Gallup poll found that over 65 percent of doctors surveyed had been involved in decisions to disconnect life-support equipment. Other polls show that the general public has formed a consensus that this practice is acceptable. Fourteen years after the Quinlan ruling, this consensus was tested in a case involving not the unplugging of a respirator, but the withdrawal of a feeding tube. This case made it all the way to the U.S. Supreme Court.

The Case of Nancy Cruzan: Passive Euthanasia Reaches the Supreme Court

On January 11, 1983, the Rambler that twenty-five-year-old Nancy Cruzan[4] was driving went out of control on an icy road in Missouri and rolled over several times. Nancy landed facedown in a ditch, where she could not breathe. The efforts of a paramedic kept Nancy alive after her heart had stopped, but rescue workers did not arrive in time to save her from irreversible brain damage caused by suffocation.

Like Karen Quinlan, Nancy lapsed into a persistent vegetative state, although she was not placed on a respirator. She was eventually moved to the Missouri Rehabilitation Center, although there was no question of "rehabilitation." The only life support she needed was a thin tube, surgically implanted above her navel, that reached into her digestive tract. Three times daily her

21

nurses fed her canned liquid nutrients through the device.

Nancy was the second of three daughters raised by Joe Cruzan, a sheet-metal worker, and Joyce Cruzan, a secretary. She grew up in Carterville, Missouri, a pretty and popular teenager more involved with her social life than with academics. In high school she played the flute and twirled a baton with the band. She was married twice and had various jobs in succession—as a waitress, a cashier, and a worker in a cheese plant. Her father described her as "proud and independent."

After the accident, her family hoped Nancy might recover. They tried everything, even bringing her home for Christmas, hoping that being among things she knew would somehow jolt her mind back. The Cruzans celebrated the holiday with Nancy in their living room, but she was oblivious, and she was brought back to the hospital with no improvement.

Reports of the costs of Nancy's care ranged from $75,000 to $100,000 each year. When her health insurance ran out after two and a half years, the government paid these costs.

After Nancy had been unconscious for two years, it became clear her condition was deteriorating. Her family considered the options. Christy, one of her sisters, remembered that after her ill grandmother died, Nancy said this was for the best if the woman couldn't live fully. The family discussed what Nancy would have wanted,

Nancy Cruzan opening gifts on Christmas morning, December 1982, just three weeks before the car accident that resulted in her falling into a "persistent vegetative state."

and, according to Joe Cruzan, they decided that keeping her alive would be more selfish than letting her die.

The only way to let her die that would possibly be legal, though, would be to have doctors remove the feeding tube through which she received nutrition and fluid. This would mean Nancy would die of starvation and dehydration. When neurologists told the Cruzans that Nancy would not feel any pain from this, because in her state she could not feel anything, they decided to go ahead with it.

As in the Quinlan case, the hospital refused. They wouldn't honor the Cruzans' request without a court order. Part of the problem was that denying a patient food and water is more controversial than turning off a respirator. Donald Lamkins, the hospital director, later said, "We know we can unplug a machine. That isn't nearly so hard for us to accept. But . . . starve somebody to death? We don't do that."

In this view nutrition is a form of basic human care, not medical care. While respirators might count as "extraordinary" treatment because people do not ordinarily rely on them—they breathe on their own—many people, such as children and those who are paralyzed, do depend on others to feed them every day. Neglecting to do this is considered deplorable and often criminal.

But many medical organizations, including the American Medical Association, consider artificial feeding a form of medical treatment similar to the respirator. They argue that just as people don't naturally breathe using a machine, they don't naturally "eat" by getting chemical nutrients through an implanted tube. Both are technological, intrusive means of care, and can be considered "extraordinary" for some patients.

Nancy's nurses, who believed that she sometimes was aware, were also against ending the feeding. One of them said she had seen Nancy laugh at jokes and turn when she heard her name. "There are times when she is totally unresponsive, and there are times when her eyes are crystal clear. She is there."

But medical evidence contradicted this possibility, and Joe Cruzan, who had spent much time looking and hoping for such responses, had to dismiss it. The reactions the nurse described, he said, were merely reflexes. Still, Joyce Cruzan said she and Joe would sometimes talk to Nancy, even knowing they weren't being heard: "It's for our benefit, not hers. It's kind of a game we play with ourselves."

The Cruzans began their four-year history-making legal journey to end Nancy's life. During their quest her father said, "As far as we're concerned, our daughter is dead. But we haven't been allowed to bury her. There's always the thought that I'll wake up, that it is all a bad dream. But I never do."

First they brought their case to a county trial court. There was testimony that Nancy had had a "somewhat serious conversation" when she was twenty-five with a friend in which she said "she would not wish to continue her life unless she could live at least halfway normally." Judge Charles Teel, Jr., satisfied that Nancy "would not wish to continue with nutrition and hydration," ruled that the feeding tube could be removed.

The state of Missouri appealed to the Missouri supreme court, arguing, among other things, that withholding food and water amounted to murder. In a 4–3 decision, the higher court ruled in favor of the state. Nancy might have a right to refuse treatment if she could make her wishes clear, but the evidence of her wishes, the justices said, was not strong enough.

The opinion by Judge Edward Robertson, Jr., noted that the state had passed an antiabortion law in 1986 saying, "Missouri adopts a strong predisposition in favor of preserving life." Because of this bias toward life, the court required that the evidence presented about Nancy's wishes be extremely persuasive: in legal terms, it must be "clear and convincing." But the court found the evidence presented to be unreliable.

Robertson wrote that Nancy's poor quality of life was irrelevant: "Were quality of life at issue, persons with all manner of handicaps might find the state seeking to terminate their lives." He also stated that tube feeding could not be considered extraordinary medical care: "Common sense tells us that food and water do not treat an illness, they maintain a life."

The Supreme Court Decision in *Missouri* v. *Cruzan*

The Cruzans appealed to the U.S. Supreme Court, which handed down a 5–4 ruling on June 25, 1990. By now, Nancy had been unconscious for more than seven years. Chief Justice William Rehnquist wrote the majority opinion, which said the case presented "a perplexing question with unusually strong moral and ethical overtones." The Court indicated that there is a constitutional right to refuse medical treatment even if death results. It also did not distinguish between artificial nutrition and hydration and other forms of medical treatment.

Nevertheless, the Court ruled against the Cruzans and in favor of Missouri. It said that though they did not have to, states *could* require "clear and convincing evidence" of what an unconscious patient would have wanted before allowing the withdrawal of care. This would help ensure that patients would not be deprived of care against their wishes. The ruling encouraged the use of advance directives (discussed later), by which people could indicate in advance what they would want for themselves should they end up in a condition like Nancy Cruzan's. These statements would count as "clear and convincing" evidence.

The four dissenting justices believed that the Cruzans should have been allowed to decide for Nancy and saw this ruling as a grave violation of the whole family's constitutional rights. In his dissent, Justice John Paul Stevens wrote:

> There can be no doubt that [Nancy's] life made her dear to her family, and to others. How she dies will affect how that life is remembered. The trial court's order authorizing Nancy's parents to cease their daughter's treatment would have permitted the family that cares for Nancy to bring to a close her tragedy and her death. Missouri's objection to that order subordinates Nancy's body, her family, and the lasting significance of her life to the State's own interests.[5]

The state's interests in her life were weak, said Stevens, because "for patients like Nancy Cruzan, who have no consciousness and no chance of recovery, there is a serious question as to whether the mere persistence of their bodies is 'life' as that word is commonly understood, or as it is used in both the Constitution and the Declaration of Independence."[6]

Despite their rebuff from the land's highest court, the Cruzans did not give up their fight. Their lawyer got the "clear and convincing" evidence they needed and went back to the original trial court. Three witnesses told of specific discussions in which Nancy said she would not want to live "like a vegetable." This time when Judge Teel ruled for the Cruzans, the state did not appeal. Two hours later her feeding tube was removed; she died on December 26, 1990.

Her father said, "Hundreds of thousands of people can rest free, knowing that when death beckons they can meet it face-to-face with dignity. I think this is quite an accomplishment [for Nancy], and I'm damn proud of her." But some people disagreed. Nancy Myers of the National Right to Life Committee said Teel's decision "represents a serious decline in how our society values human life," and one of Cruzan's nurses remarked bitterly, "The Humane Society won't let you starve your dog."

The Supreme Court ruling in the Cruzan case was a mixed one for advocates on both sides of the issue. On the one hand, the Court allowed states to make it difficult for family members to have care withdrawn from an unconscious patient. On the other, the Court did not *require* states to do this, so courts and legislatures in the individual states were free to make treatment withdrawal easy. Only two other states—New York and Maine—take the kind of position that Missouri took during the Cruzan case; the other states have far less stringent requirements. In January 1993 Missouri's new attorney general announced that the state would no longer interefere with treatment withdrawal decisions made by families of vegetative patients.

A few months before the Supreme Court ruling in the Cruzan case, the *New York Times* and CBS News conducted a poll in which people were asked if close family members of unconscious patients should have the right to end their tube feeding.[7] Of those polled, 81 percent said yes, while 13 percent said no. When asked what they would want for themselves in this situation, 85 percent opted for the tube to be removed, while 11 percent did not. This lopsided public opinion makes it unlikely that many state legislatures will pass laws interfering with the right to die. Indeed, after *Cruzan,* the U.S. Congress passed a law advancing this right by encouraging the use of advance directives.

Meanwhile, the Catholic Church remains divided on the withdrawal of treatment from permanently unconscious patients. In April 1992 a committee of the nation's Roman Catholic bishops issued a statement acknowledging this division, but it went on to warn the public about what they considered the dangerous precedent of allowing treatment withdrawal:

> We are gravely concerned about current attitudes and policy trends in our society that would too easily dismiss patients without apparent mental faculties as nonpersons or as undeserving of human care and concern.[8]

The bishops feared that society might come to see people with a broad range of physical and mental disabilities as not having lives worth living. They also worried that passive euthanasia would lead to active euthanasia.

The Cruzan case stirred a new debate among medical ethicists over the definition of death. The debate was also influenced by the case of a Florida baby born in March 1992 with anencephaly—she had no brain except for the primitive brain stem. She did not have long to live, and her parents wanted to donate her organs to aid other infants with medical problems before she died and her organs broke down. But they were not allowed to remove the organs because legally, the baby was still alive.

Medical ethicist John Fletcher argued that people who have no higher brain functions—PVS patients and anencephalic babies—should be considered legally dead: "The death of the higher brain is the death of what makes us human." Others were not comfortable with this suggestion, noting that using total brain death as the legal definition of death was safer—it ensured that no one who could recover from his condition would be declared dead. Further, as ethicist and neurologist Dr. Ronald Cranford put it, "It is pretty horrifying and psychologically jarring, to say the least, to look at someone whose eyes are open and say they are dead."[9]

One Solution: The Advance Directive

Advance directives are legal forms in which a person says what kind of care she wants should she become hopelessly ill and unable to communicate her treatment desires. Though they have been in use in some states since the 1970s, the documents became the focus of greater public interest in the wake of the tragic case of

A married couple, Seth and Sara Faison, discuss their concerns before filling out health care advance directives.

Nancy Cruzan. With the Supreme Court deciding that they could serve as crucial legal evidence of what an unconscious patient would have wanted—and with many people dreading the idea of having their life maintained indefinitely by medical equipment—advance directives looked like a promising way out of a dilemma.

There are two kinds of advance directives: one, usually called a "living will," specifies what kind of medical treatment a person wants or doesn't want to receive should she become critically ill. For instance, someone might direct doctors not to use a respirator to keep her alive if she will die soon anyway. The other, often called a "health care proxy," allows someone to designate another trusted person to make this type of decision for her. Every U.S. state has a law recognizing at least one form of advance directive.

During the six months following the decision in *Missouri* v. *Cruzan* , the group Choice in Dying received 800,000 requests for advance-directive forms. A copy of the form they supply, which includes both a living will and a health care proxy, is shown on pages 34 and 35. (Forms are available from Choice in Dying, Inc. See "For Further Information" on page 108 for address.) The group says that about one-fifth of the U.S. population has completed an advance directive.

Also in the wake of the Cruzan case, Congress passed the Patient Self-Determination Act to foster the use of advance directives. The law requires federally funded

ADVANCE DIRECTIVE
Living Will and Health Care Proxy

D *eath is a part of life. It is a reality like birth, growth and aging. I am using this advance directive to convey my wishes about medical care to my doctors and other people looking after me at the end of my life. It is called an advance directive because it gives instructions in advance about what I want to happen to me in the future. It expresses my wishes about medical treatment that might keep me alive. I want this to be legally binding.*

If I cannot make or communicate decisions about my medical care, those around me should rely on this document for instructions about measures that could keep me alive.

I do not want medical treatment (including feeding and water by tube) that will keep me alive if:
 • I am unconscious and there is no reasonable prospect that I will ever be conscious again (even if I am not going to die soon in my medical condition), <u>or</u>
 • I am near death from an illness or injury with no reasonable prospect of recovery.

I do want medicine and other care to make me more comfortable and to take care of pain and suffering. I want this even if the pain medicine makes me die sooner.

I want to give some extra instructions: [*Here list any special instructions, e.g., some people fear being kept alive after a debilitating stroke. If you have wishes about this, or any other conditions, please write them here.*]

The legal language in the box that follows is a health care proxy.
It gives another person the power to make medical decisions for me.

I name _____, who lives at _____

_____, phone number _____,

to make medical decisions for me if I cannot make them myself. This person is called a health care "surrogate," "agent," "proxy," or "attorney in fact." This power of attorney shall become effective when I become incapable of making or communicating decisions about my medical care. This means that this document stays legal when and if I lose the power to speak for myself, for instance, if I am in a coma or have Alzheimer's disease.

My health care proxy has power to tell others what my advance directive means. This person also has power to make decisions for me, based either on what I would have wanted, or, if this is not known, on what he or she thinks is best for me.

If my first choice health care proxy cannot or decides not to act for me, I name _____

_____, address _____,

phone number _____, as my second choice.

(continued on other side)

I have discussed my wishes with my health care proxy, and with my second choice if I have chosen to appoint a second person. My proxy(ies) has(have) agreed to act for me.

I have thought about this advance directive carefully. I know what it means and want to sign it. I have chosen two witnesses, neither of whom is a member of my family, nor will inherit from me when I die. My witnesses are not the same people as those I named as my health care proxies. I understand that this form should be notarized if I use the box to name (a) health care proxy(ies).

Signature _____

Date _____

Address _____

Witness' signature _____

Witness' printed name _____

Address _____

Witness' signature _____

Witness' printed name _____

Address _____

Notary [to be used if proxy is appointed] _____

Drafted and distributed by Choice In Dying, Inc.—the national council for the right to die. Choice In Dying is a national not-for-profit organization which works for the rights of patients at the end of life. In addition to this generic advance directive, Choice In Dying distributes advance directives that conform to each state's specific legal requirements and maintains a national Living Will Registry for completed documents.

CHOICE IN DYING, INC.—
the national council for the right to die
(formerly Concern for Dying/Society for the Right to Die)
200 Varick Street, New York, NY 10014 (212) 366-5540

hospitals and nursing homes to tell patients over eighteen that they have the right to plan ahead by filling out a living will or a health care proxy. Institutions devise their own procedures for complying with the requirement. At one Chicago hospital, before a patient is admitted a clerk asks her or him, "Do you have a living will? Can we have a copy of it?" Patients without directives receive literature explaining Illinois law regarding living wills.

While many experts welcome the use of advance directives—an editorial in the *Journal of the American Medical Association (JAMA)* said they "will greatly assist clinicians, patients and family members . . . with increasingly complex health care decision making"[10]— they are not without their problems. One difficulty is that it is impossible to imagine in advance all the different ways in which you could become ill and how aggressively you would want to be treated under different circumstances. The *JAMA* editorial acknowledged that living wills may be "vague and imprecise" and "subject to interpretation" by doctors.

And other *JAMA* writers worried that one result of the new federal living-will law would be that "patients who are illiterate, medically indigent, or unaware of advance directives' significance may be asked to make choices about which they have little understandable information."[11]

Because of various problems with living wills, some

Seth Faison signs an advance directive.

experts recommend that people appoint a health care proxy instead of, or in addition to, signing a living will. They say that people should discuss with their proxies what kind of care they would wish to receive if they became incapacitated. Of course, this suggestion does not help those who are alone in the world and thus have no one they trust who can fill the role of proxy.

For those with a sanctity-of-life perspective, the National Right to Life Committee has produced a counterpoint to the standard advance directive. Called a "will to live," this document (available from National Right to Life, address in "For Further Information") instructs doctors never to deny the person food or fluids, and it says:

> I request and direct that medical treatment and care be provided to me to preserve my life without discrimination based on my age or physical or mental disability or the "quality" of my life. I reject any action or omission that is intended to cause or hasten my death.

3

Some Other Dilemmas

Infants in Intensive Care: To Treat or Not to Treat?

Babies, of course, cannot fill out living wills or make medical decisions for themselves. Critically ill infants lie helplessly in incubators while parents, doctors, and, sometimes, courts determine their fate. They also lie at the heart of another debate over passive euthanasia.[1]

Babies born prematurely—well in advance of the usual nine-month period of pregnancy—and underweight are especially at risk for serious health problems. Not that long ago most of them died quickly. But the development of newborn intensive care in the early 1960s saved younger and younger infants, with lower and lower birth weights. Being born prematurely no longer necessarily meant facing death.

More recently, the development of artificial wombs has increased survival rates so dramatically that in the period from 1981 to 1985, 48 percent of newborns weighing under 2 pounds, 3 ounces survived. Between 1961 and 1975, only *6 percent* of such babies lived!

The scene where some of these infants are cared for is described by Howard W. French:

> In a special section of the neonatal intensive-care ward, where the most dangerously premature children are kept, babies hardly larger than a hand are cared for by teams of nurses. Each is connected to a gaggle of monitoring devices. Gold heart-shaped thermometers; respirator tubes in tracheas; laser blood-oxygen sensors attached to feet; pulse-measuring gauges on chests; and the ubiquitous intravenous tubing that provides both nutrition and medication.[2]

For the babies who will survive and have a good quality of life, such care is clearly a blessing. For others, who may be suffering and have no real chance of surviving more than a short while, it may instead be cruel. Half the survivors of infant intensive care will be disabled all their lives. It is often difficult to say, however, what the outcome will be for an infant: Sometimes a baby thought to be in a hopeless condition improves, and sometimes a baby expected to get better does not.

Doctors used to act to prevent suffering by withholding extraordinary medical treatment from some newborns. At one hospital in the early 1970s, for instance, of 299 infants who died over a certain period, 43 with birth defects had been allowed to die by doctors, with the permission of the parents.[3]

But this practice was sharply curtailed in the mid-1980s, as a result of several publicized cases that outraged many people. In one, a baby cared for in a hospital in Bloomington, Indiana, had a birth defect—a blockage in the esophagus—that prevented it from eating normally. Apparently because the baby also had Down syndrome, a form of mental retardation, the parents would not let doctors correct the esophageal defect. The hospital asked a court for permission to perform the surgery over the parents' wishes, but the court refused, saying the parents' decision was protected by their right to privacy. The baby died at six days of age.

Some people were angry that children in these situations were being allowed to die. They pointed out that retarded people can have meaningful lives in spite of their disability, and argued that withholding treatment from them is a form of discrimination against the handicapped. As a result, federal regulations were passed requiring treatment for disabled children unless they are also in a coma or terminally ill.

Partly because of these regulations, doctors have

become much more aggressive in their treatment of sick infants, even if that causes a conflict with the infants' parents. One survey, taken in Massachusetts in 1988, showed doctors to treat more aggressively and with less regard for what parents wanted than they did when surveyed in 1977. Some people feel that whereas doctors used to undertreat, they now overtreat. The result are stories like that of Jan Anderson of Minneapolis.

Twenty-three weeks into Anderson's pregnancy, she gave birth to a 1-pound 5-ounce boy, whom she named Aaron. While the boy was in intensive care, she felt he was suffering greatly and that his future did not look promising. She asked Aaron's doctors to disconnect his respirator. They would not consider this option, and one of them, she said, "would scream at me, 'We're going to save your child, not kill him.' "

Aaron did survive. But he was paralyzed below the neck, virtually blind, had cerebral palsy, and was possibly mentally retarded. While his mother "loves Aaron and has devoted her life to caring for him," according to the report in the *New York Times,* she does not think he should have been "saved." "There's no need for anyone to suffer like this," she says.

On the question of passive euthanasia, or withdrawal of treatment, the recent trend in the care of critically ill babies runs in the opposite direction from the trend in the care of very sick or unconscious adults. The former are treated far more aggressively than the latter. One problem with this is economic: The United States spends $2.6 billion on neonatal intensive care each year.

Some experts, like bioethicist Daniel Callahan, say we have our priorities backward. He argues that it would make more sense to increase spending on care for mothers before they give birth. If more mothers got good prenatal care, fewer babies would be born prematurely, and so we could spend less on high-tech care for unhealthy infants.

Severely Disabled Adults

In 1985 Larry James McAfee of Georgia broke his neck in a motorcycle accident.[4] He was paralyzed from the neck down and needed a respirator to stay alive. For a year after the accident he lived in a rehabilitation center for people with spinal cord injuries. Private insurance allowed him to live and be cared for in his own Atlanta apartment for about a year after that. But when the insurance was exhausted, he had to move to a nursing home because state funds would not pay for his care elsewhere. After being sent to a nursing home in Ohio and a hospital in Atlanta, he ended up in a nursing home in Alabama.

The *New York Times* described McAfee as having "the build of a football player" and, before the accident, being "an avid outdoorsman who lived to hunt and to ride his motorcycle." Now, in the typical nursing home routine, "he is cleaned, and his lungs are suctioned.

Then he [is] dressed in a jogging suit and athletic shoes and left in his wheelchair, which he moves with a breath-activated device, with little more to do than to watch television."

In 1989, at the age of thirty-three, McAfee decided his paralyzed condition, known as quadriplegia, made his life not worth living. He did not enjoy life and felt his total dependency on others to be "demeaning" and "draining."

McAfee tried to dislodge his respirator so he could die, but the awful suffocating feeling he experienced prevented him from doing so. To successfully remove the respirator, he would need someone to give him a sedative, which would allow him to die peacefully. But the hospital he was in at the time refused to comply with this request. So McAfee went to court, seeking authorization for the removal of the machine that kept him alive.

Cases in which severely disabled people go to court seeking to disconnect their own life-support systems are rarer than right-to-die cases brought to court by the guardians of unconscious people. In both types of cases, though, only a small proportion end up in court; most of them are dealt with privately, with an agreement being reached between doctors, families, and patients. In some ways Larry McAfee's case was easier than those of Karen Quinlan or Nancy Cruzan. He was conscious and capable of making decisions himself about his health care—and people generally have the legal right to refuse treatment.

On the other hand, although McAfee's disability had ravaged his body, it left his ability to think and interact with other people intact. McAfee was capable of leading a meaningful life, and he was not terminally ill. Whether the state, through the courts, should help someone end such a life is a difficult question.

McAfee told Georgia Superior Court Judge Edward H. Johnson that he woke up every morning "fearful of each new day" and wanted to die. His family supported McAfee's request. His mother, father, and three sisters testified that he felt he no longer enjoyed life. According to one sister, "He said he did not want to exist like this. He said he wasn't living."

The judge ruled that McAfee could disconnect the respirator and receive sedatives from medical personnel to aid the process. He said he admired McAfee's courage and could not stand in the way of someone who believed his respirator "is not prolonging his life, but is instead prolonging his death."

On appeal, the judges of the Georgia supreme court unanimously upheld the ruling. They held that McAfee had the right to determine his own medical care—because in this case constitutionally protected privacy rights outweigh state interests in preserving life. Other courts have also ruled this way in similar cases, and they have also honored the wishes of disabled people to have feeding tubes removed.

The McAfee ruling was applauded by right-to-die advocates. Fenella Rouse, then director of legal services for the Society for the Right to Die (the group has since changed its name to Choice in Dying), said, "It sends chills up anyone's spine to see someone saying their life is not acceptable and they want to end it, but the law is clear that people have the right to decide what level of medical care they want to receive."

Four organizations for disabled people, however, deplored the decision and issued a statement saying that it placed a low value on the lives of disabled people. Paul K. Longmore, a historian and a quadriplegic who has used a respirator for over twenty-five years, said that McAfee's "despairing choice is not simply a reaction to the hardship of a physical disability." Rather, it reflected society's failure to make it possible for people with disabilities to lead meaningful lives.

Longmore noted that McAfee's home state of Georgia doesn't pay for "independent living" programs that enable severely disabled people to live in their own homes. He said:

> By failing over the past several years to let him exercise his right to independent living and self-determination—his right to work, to society, to life—the state of Georgia in effect has been

telling Larry McAfee, 'People like you are better off dead.' He got the message.[5]

Events after the Georgia supreme court's decision seemed to support Longmore's argument that people like McAfee need not die, if only someone would take an interest in their lives. In an ironic twist, the court case created publicity that gave McAfee new options. A doctor introduced him to United Cerebral Palsy of Greater Birmingham, which offers a program that helps severely disabled people become employed, and McAfee began computer training. He said, "Turning off the ventilator [respirator] still remains a very viable option to me. But I want to look into the possibilities to see what's available first. I want to give it a try."

But apparently not all disabled people who want to end their lives are the victims of indifference or discrimination. In his book *Final Exit* (discussed further in Chapter 5), Derek Humphry tells the story of James Haig, who, at age twenty-four, was transformed by a motorcycle accident "from an active sportsman and husband and father into an 84-pound quadriplegic."[6] The accident left Haig with some use of his fingers, with which he could operate an electric wheelchair.

He tried to adjust to his condition for four years, during which he received excellent medical care as well as extensive psychological counseling. His accident insurance provided sufficient funds to live on. But according to Humphry, "Despite all the care, love and money that had been lavished on him, he said he simply could not live in this smashed condition."

Haig was determined to kill himself. He first tried to drown himself by driving his wheelchair into a river, but he got stuck in the mud. Then a friend agreed to provide him with lethal drugs but backed out of the plan. Finally, he set fire to his house and remained inside, and this killed him.

II

Active Euthanasia and Assisted Suicide

4

The Lethal Dose

Some terminally ill patients who are perfectly alert may want to die before their disease can progress any further. They may have cancer and be in pain; they may suffer from a debilitating ailment like Alzheimer's disease and face the prospect of mental deterioration and helplessness in the future; they may be afflicted by the ravages of AIDS. In situations in which it is not possible to end their lives quickly and without great pain by refusing treatment, many patients commit suicide.

Government records show that the suicide rate among Americans aged sixty-five years and older increased 25 percent between 1981 and 1986. Some experts speculate that this is a result of advances in health care that keep people alive longer—but with a quality of life they may find unacceptable. Facing incurable diseases like Alzheimer's and knowing the high cost of health care, people may feel suicide is their only option.

Some patients who want to commit suicide seek the assistance of a physician or a loved one, asking him or her, for instance, to provide a lethal dose of sleeping pills. Depending on where a patient lives, it may be clearly illegal to comply with such a request: While suicide is legal in this country, assisting a suicide is outlawed by legislation in a majority of states.

To help a patient who wants to die painlessly, a doctor may also give a lethal injection of drugs. This practice, called "active voluntary euthanasia"—known more informally as "mercy killing"—is a crime through-out the United States and all other countries.

While the most controversial treatment-withdrawal cases have involved vegetative patients like Karen Quinlan and Nancy Cruzan, the patients in active euthanasia and assisted suicide cases are conscious and express a wish to end their life. As far as the law is concerned, it makes no difference if euthanasia is requested by the person who wishes to die, the patient is suffering greatly, or his condition is hopeless—it is none-theless illegal.

Still, in the United States no doctor has ever been prosecuted for assisting a suicide, and juries have been reluctant to convict as murderers people who took part in the mercy killing of a loved one. Later in Part II we will look at cases in which family members and doctors have helped people to die.

Some of the pro-and-con arguments used in the debate over active euthanasia overlap those regarding passive euthanasia. Many people in this country, including most medical ethicists, favor passive euthanasia but are opposed to active euthanasia. They believe there is a fine moral line between the latter, which they consider to be "killing," and the former, which they consider to be "letting die." (Assisted suicide seems to occupy a moral middle ground.) Others see passive and active euthanasia as morally equivalent, because both intend to cause death, and either support or oppose both practices.

The American Medical Association opposes active euthanasia and assisted suicide, as do most major U.S. religious groups. This opposition has historic roots: The Hippocratic oath, an ethical code from ancient Greece that some doctors still swear to, says, "I will neither give a deadly drug to anybody if asked for it, nor will I make a suggestion to this effect." Judeo-Christian law thousands of years old contains strict prohibitions against both killing and suicide.

Some people who support the right to die, and who believe that this includes the right to a physician's aid in dying, are working to legalize active voluntary euthanasia and assisted suicide in the United States. A group called the Hemlock Society was founded in 1980 to advance this cause. The following are some of the main arguments put forward by advocates of active euthanasia, followed by rebuttals from opponents of the practice. Keep these arguments in mind as you read the case studies in Chapters 5 and 6.

The Case for Legalizing Active Euthanasia and Assisted Suicide

- Suicide often results from emotional problems, as when a teenager who is depressed and alienated from his parents takes his life. We should all try to prevent this from occurring. But there is another kind of suicide, which we should allow. It is possible for people who are terminally ill and suffering—whether physically, emotionally, or spiritually—to make a reasoned decision that life is no longer worth living. They may feel that they can't do the things that once made life meaningful to them or that death is preferable to the pain of their existence. Their decision to end their lives is known as rational suicide.

- The philosophy behind a democracy is that the state exists to serve individuals, rather than the other way around. The respect given to individuals in a democracy, the recognition of their inherent worth and dignity, means (1) that they should not be forced to suffer unnecessarily, and (2) that they have self-determination—the freedom to do whatever they want to do, including decide when and how they die, as long as they don't hurt anyone else. Therefore, euthanasia, an individual act hurting no one else, should be permitted. In the words of advocate Derek Humphry, euthanasia is "the ultimate civil liberty."

- No one is suggesting that people opposed to euthanasia choose it for themselves. But these people don't have the right to dictate their values—including their religious beliefs—to others with different outlooks, who do want to die this way. Secular democracies should not be governed by religious law.

- Doctors opposed to euthanasia should not be required to carry it out. Some doctors, however, see it as their duty to help suffering, hopeless people who request the relief of death. They say euthanasia would be an extension of the care they provided to terminally ill patients to make the remainder of their life as comfortable as possible. Doctors should be able to fulfill this moral and professional obligation without fear of legal prosecution.

- While pain can often be treated with drugs, in some cases medication is inadequate or unavailable and a terminally ill patient suffers greatly. For such a patient, active euthanasia can provide a much-wished-for release. Also, painkillers themselves may induce a stupor or unconsciousness—states in which the patient may not wish to live.

- Suffering is not confined to physical pain. When a patient has a debilitating disease that robs him of his dignity because he cannot control his bowels or bladder, or he is very dependent on others because he must be fed or cleaned by them, he may suffer intensely and rationally prefer death.

- It is a great comfort to people to know that euthanasia is an option, even if they do not use it. They know that if their suffering becomes unbearable, they have an escape. For some people, having this control over their death allows them to get more out of the time they have left.

6 moe conclusion

- While hospices, facilities set up specifically to provide a caring environment for the terminally ill, are good at what they do, they do not solve all the problems faced by these patients. For instance, if a person greatly valued being active and his illness makes him bedridden, a hospice could not change this. Hospices thus are not for everyone. Some people would prefer not to linger in a hospice, and they should have the option of ending their life sooner.

- Legal safeguards can prevent euthanasia from being abused. For instance, in the Netherlands, where euthanasia is allowed although technically illegal, guidelines provide that patients must be hopelessly ill, in unrelievable pain or discomfort, are rational and fully informed, and ask for death several times. Two doctors must agree to go along with the patient's wishes.

The Case Against Legalizing Active Euthanasia and Assisted Suicide

- Euthanasia is wrong in principle. Prohibitions against killing are a bedrock of civilization, and there should be no exceptions. In the religious view, upholding the biblical commandment "Thou shalt not kill" is vital to our collective survival. Life is for the Creator, not people, to take, and doctors who perform euthanasia are "playing God."

- A policy allowing euthanasia presumes that the elderly, the weak, the disabled, and people who are seriously ill would be better off dead and society would be better off without them. This callous, shallow outlook degrades our humanity and fails to appreciate the value of every individual.

- Euthanasia would be subject to several forms of abuse: (1) Family members, tired of taking care of a terminally ill person or paying for his care, might encourage him to request euthanasia, and he might feel obligated to comply so as not to be a "burden." (2) Doctors would have great power, both because of their professional authority and the terminally ill patient's condition. Whether out of self-interest or a genuine desire to relieve suffering, they could persuade a patient to request euthanasia who would not otherwise have done so. (3) The U.S. health care system is in crisis and the cost of care is soaring. If euthanasia were legal, hospitals, nursing homes, and insurance companies anxious to cut costs would be tempted to make it the most desirable option, or the only available one, in cases where a patient's treatment was expensive.

- Euthanasia could well be the first slide down a "slippery slope" leading to the complete moral breakdown of society. It would start with people being *helped* to die; then they would be *encouraged* to die; then they would be *pressured* to die; and finally they would be *forced* to die—involuntary euthanasia. At first euthanasia would be used only for the terminally ill, then it might be expanded to the chronically ill, then the disabled, and finally to despised racial groups. The Nazis began their genocidal drive for racial purity with a propaganda campaign to allow euthanasia of the severely ill. Eventually people who were unproductive, or dissidents, or racially "impure," or, finally, just not German were considered unworthy to live.

- What appears to be "rational suicide" may actually be highly irrational because the decision is due to temporary depression rather than any logic. Depression is a psychological condition in which a person experiences a deep despair and hopelessness. It can often be treated independently of the patient's illness. In some cases a terminally ill person may plan a suicide, then changes his mind when his depression lifts and his outlook gets brighter. The time left before he succumbs to his disease may now hold great meaning for him.

- In almost all cases, pain can be treated with drugs. If techniques for controlling pain were improved even more, and if these techniques were always available, few people would want active euthanasia for themselves. If euthanasia were legalized and accepted as a way out, doctors would not work as hard to alleviate their patients' pain. Euthanasia advocates would do better to channel their energy into fighting for improved pain control.

- Hospices are a healthy alternative to euthanasia. They provide comfort, security, love, and dignity to patients who are not attached to machines to keep them alive. Hospice patients do not wish to commit suicide.

- A doctor's role is to heal, not to kill. If doctors were allowed to kill through active euthanasia, it would undermine the trust in the profession that physicians need to have to do their job.

- There is a distinction between private morality and public policy: Though certain individual cases of active euthanasia might be morally justifiable, this does not mean that the practice should be legal. The widespread practice of euthanasia could be highly destructive to society. It might result in abuses, a decreased respect for human life, and an erosion of the doctor-patient relationship.

5

Aiding the Death of a Loved One

Betty Rollin Grants Her Mother's "Last Wish"

In the spring of 1981 New York television newswoman Betty Rollin was shocked to learn that her seventy-three-year-old mother, Ida, had ovarian cancer.[1] Although she had had cancer herself, Rollin, Ida's only daughter, never thought her mother would develop it. Ida's doctors prescribed a grueling course of chemotherapy, and Rollin was surprised again—this time by what Ida was willing to go through to live.

According to Rollin, life had treated Ida well. She was a devoted mother and had been a devoted wife until her husband died. She had many friends. Ida was

Betty Rollin with her mother, Ida, in 1978. Rollin's book *Last Wish*, about how she helped Ida to die, brought the issue of assisted suicide to a mass audience in a very personal way.

grateful for her good fortune, and her daughter called her "the world's most cheerful person." When she learned that she had cancer, she exhibited no fear or self-pity.

For eight months Ida went to the hospital the first weekend of every month and received cancer-fighting drugs intravenously. The treatments made her vomit every fifteen minutes and sapped her strength. Her hair fell out. Rollin describes finding her in the hospital "half dead, her shoulders rounded, her body slumped as if the bones had been removed, too weak by far to walk."

Finally the treatments were over, and Ida could get back to her life. She resumed taking folk-dancing classes, and in September 1982 she celebrated her seventy-fifth birthday.

But the cancer was back by June 1983, and it was inoperable. Ida's doctor recommended more chemotherapy, and she agreed to do it. Rollin said, "I thought, 'Oh, my God, is she going to put herself through this hell again?' But she wanted to live."

This time, though, she could not tolerate the chemotherapy. With an untreatable, growing tumor interfering with her digestive system and causing her pain, Ida's prospects were gloomy. The doctor told Rollin her mother probably had only several months more to live.

At this point for Ida, that was too long. She said to Rollin, "To me, this isn't life. Life is taking a walk, visiting my children, eating!" She also said, "I'm not afraid to die, but I am afraid of this illness, what it's doing to me." She asked for her daughter's assistance in ending her life.

Though hesitant at first, when Rollin was sure that her mother really wanted this, she agreed to help.

But how? There were no easy answers. Rollin discussed different possibilities with her husband: car exhaust, arsenic, cyanide, a gun. The only method that made sense to them, though, was to use prescription drugs. To do this correctly, they would need to learn from a doctor the type of drugs and dosages that would do the job, and how Ida should take them. But medical professionals, for legal or ethical reasons, would not tell them anything. Eventually they found a European doctor, a euthanasia supporter, willing to give them the information they were seeking.

They began planning the suicide. One day when Rollin started crying, Ida reassured her, saying, "I'm lucky I can get out of this. The people I feel sorry for are all the people who want to and can't." On another occasion Ida said she was thankful she could think clearly so she could make this decision.

October 17, 1983, was the day. Ida made sure her finances were in order. She put on lipstick. When Rollin and her husband arrived at her apartment, the three of them looked at family photo albums for a while, then it was time. As Ida swallowed the pills, Rollin whispered, "You're doing it, Mother. You're doing great."

While she was waiting for them to take effect, Ida said, "I want you to know that I am a happy woman. . . . I've had a wonderful life. I've had everything that is important to me. I have given love and I have received it." Soon she fell asleep. Rollin began to sob—but not for long, because her mother looked peaceful.

In the years since Ida's death, Rollin has not developed any regrets about her role in it. She was not investigated by law-enforcement officials, but occasionally someone will call her a murderer. She counters with the statement that her mother made a rational decision and that "suicide was her last wish." She says she loved Ida dearly and did not want her to die.

Rollin has become an advocate for doctor-assisted suicide, believing that laws should permit physicians to help sick people who want to die. "You shouldn't have to count on a child to do this," she says. She told the story of her mother's death in the book *Last Wish*, and more recently she wrote the foreword to *Final Exit*, a suicide manual discussed later in this chapter. She says she's received many letters from people in situations like her mother's, some of whom "have tried to die, failed, and suffered even more."

She sums up her pro-euthanasia views this way: "Some people want to eke out every second of life, no matter how grim, and that is their right. But others do not, and that should be *their* right. Until it is, people who want a safe, peaceful exit and can't get it will continue to suffer."

Euthanasia at Gunpoint: The Story of Roswell Gilbert

For many years Roswell Gilbert and his wife, Emily, were happily married and led a wonderful life together.[2]

They were both attractive people, and his successful career as an electronics engineer gave them enough money to live well. A friend of theirs remarked that she had never seen two people so devoted to each other.

In 1978, when they were both in their sixties, they moved to an apartment in Fort Lauderdale, Florida. Soon their good life began to change. Emily started forgetting obvious things like where she was going or what she had done the day before. Doctors eventually diagnosed Alzheimer's disease (see below).

Alzheimer's Disease

Alzheimer's is an irreversible, terminal disease in which the deterioration of brain tissue leads to senility. Symptoms, such as confusion and memory loss, are mild at first and worsen gradually over a period of ten or fifteen years or longer. Eventually the patient becomes completely demented and cannot take care of herself at all. Others must feed, clean, diaper, and bathe her.

About four million Americans, most of them over 65, suffer from this devastating disorder, which is the fourth leading cause of death in the nation. No one knows what causes Alzheimer's, and there is no cure for it. It is difficult to diagnose with certainty until the patient has died and an autopsy is performed.

With the passage of time, Emily grew more and more disoriented. She would fail to recognize her husband, asking him "Who are you?" every day. She would forget what state she lived in, and sometimes she would repeat a question as many as twenty times.

She also suffered from osteoporosis, an often painful condition in which the bones become brittle, and was continually being hospitalized with broken bones. Eventually her weight fell to eighty pounds. When she was in the hospital she would bother the other patients.

At home Gilbert spent much of his time taking care of his wife—feeding her, brushing her teeth, dressing her, and applying her makeup. The nursing homes he contacted refused to take her, because, they said, they could not handle a patient with Alzheimer's. And having a nurse come into their home to help Gilbert was out of the question—Emily was afraid of strangers.

On March 4, 1985, upon returning to their apartment after a difficult hospital stay, Gilbert says that Emily told him, "Ros, I love you dearly. God, I want to die." He was now seventy-five years old; she was seventy-three. They had been married almost fifty years. According to Gilbert and friends of the couple, in the past she had repeatedly expressed a desire to die. For a month, he considered granting her wish.

Finally, this March afternoon, when the sun was shining on the ocean outside their condominium, he placed his wife on a sofa. He went to his lab to get his gun, a 9-millimeter German Luger; he then shot his wife twice in the head. When the police arrived, he calmly told them what he had done.

At the trial Gilbert wouldn't apologize for shooting his wife, nor would he plead temporary insanity. He said he had done it out of love, to end her suffering. His attorney said he should not be found guilty because he had acted out of compassion. But the prosecutor called his act the "cold-blooded murder" of a person Gilbert had tired of caring for. He said that Emily was "not that bad off. She was a functioning human being. Just because someone's in pain, it doesn't mean someone else has the right to take that person's life."

The jury convicted Gilbert of first-degree (premeditated) murder, and he was sentenced to a prison term of twenty-five years. One of the jurors said, "The law does not allow for sympathy. We had to do it." The verdict and sentence were relatively harsh, though.

People rarely serve prison sentences for mercy killing. For instance, two years before the Gilbert case, a Fort Lauderdale grand jury refused to indict a different man for shooting his wife.

She had had Alzheimer's and would not stop screaming unless dosed with sedatives. Often, defendants in mercy killing cases are found not guilty by reason of temporary insanity, and those who are convicted may be sentenced to probation rather than jail time.

After the verdict Gilbert said, "I still don't feel like I

committed a crime. This just shows that the laws have to be changed."

Others disagreed. Edward R. Grant, executive director of Americans United for Life, argued that even though our emotions might favor making an exception for "compassionate" killings, the law should not bend:

> The protection of innocent human life from acts of violence is one of the fundamental purposes of our legal system. Does life become less worthy of protection when a person is old, infirm, and in need of care? If so, the assumption that the law will protect life has little meaning, for one may be asked to 'qualify' for the law's protection by meeting arbitrary physical or intellectual criteria.

When Gilbert was imprisoned at the Avon Park penitentiary in Florida, his views about the case did not change. In an interview with *50 Plus* magazine he said, "I've never been arrested before in my life, and here I am serving 25 years for the 'crime' of compassion." Asked if he thought about how he killed his wife, he nodded and said, "Every day, and every night before I go to sleep. But I always come to the same conclusion—that I did the right thing."

The prison sentence outraged many Florida residents, and a campaign was waged to grant Gilbert clemency. This attempt failed, however, until five years later, when the prosecutor in the case, Kelly Hancock, visited Gilbert in prison. He did this because the case bothered him, according to Hancock. He said that he had received hate mail about it and that he wanted to get to know Gilbert.

Seeing Gilbert—now eighty-one, frail, blind in one eye, with white hair and a host of health problems—he decided that the convict had been "punished enough." He added that this did not change his feeling that Gilbert had been guilty of a crime. Soon after that, citing information that Gilbert had heart and lung disease and was considered "at high risk of death at any time," Florida officials ordered him released from prison. Governor Bob Martinez said, "A just society is one that tempers the need for punishment with the compassion that is our hallmark as a people."

Final Exit: A Suicide Manual

Terminally ill people who want to die often cannot turn to their own doctor for medical information on ways to end their life. Assisted suicide is illegal in most of the United States, and most doctors are not trained in how to administer lethal doses. To give people access to this information, Derek Humphry, who founded the Hemlock Society in 1980 to promote the cause of legal assisted suicide and euthanasia, wrote *Final Exit: Self-Deliverance and Assisted Suicide for the Dying.* Published in 1991 by Hemlock, the suicide manual soon soared to the top of bestseller lists across the country and became, itself, a subject of heated controversy.

The book discusses such topics as how to find a

Euthanasia advocate Derek Humphry discusses his controversial suicide manual, *Final Exit: Self-Deliverance and Assisted Suicide for the Dying,* at a Hemlock Society meeting in Florida.

physician who supports your right to die (some doctors, particularly younger ones, "will discreetly prescribe lethal drugs in appropriate cases"); how to avoid legal prosecution if you help a loved one commit suicide; how to avoid an autopsy; and how to write a suicide note.

It warns readers about possibly ineffective or painful methods of committing suicide, advocating only the use of prescription drugs. It gives instructions to physicians on aiding patients with suicide and supplies a table of lethal drug dosages. And to enable you to "end your life with certainty and grace," in Humphry's words, nitty-gritty details are provided, for instance, on how to make sure you swallow all the pills—before falling asleep and without vomiting.

Humphry says of the volume:

> *Final Exit* is a book for the 1990s. . . . People today are remarkably well informed about medical problems through television, magazines and books. Personal autonomy concerning one's bodily integrity has taken hold in the public imagination. . . . Physicians are now more likely to be seen as "friendly body technicians" and no longer as the rulers of one's bodily health whose every piece of advice must be interpreted as command. *Final Exit* is aimed at helping the public and the health professional achieve death with dignity for those who desire and plan for it.[3]

Why is *Final Exit* so popular? Dr. Arthur Caplan, bioethicist at the University of Minnesota in Minneapolis, said that the high sales figures suggested "how large the issue of euthanasia looms in our society now" and that they are "the loudest statement of protest of how medicine is dealing with terminal illness and dying."[4]

Bookstore owners said buyers tended to be elderly, and often in good health. One thought that these were people who did not want to be kept alive on machines if they got sick, and they were doing advance planning.

New York Times columnist Anna Quindlen speculated that some of the people buying *Final Exit* had learned from experience what the future might hold for them if they did not plan:

> [Perhaps they had] visited nursing homes and seen people who are husks, tied upright in wheelchairs, staring at the ceiling from hospital beds, saved from death by any means possible, saved for something that is as much like life as a stone is like an egg, a twig like a finger. That is a horrid future to contemplate for those who value their strength and competence.[5]

People magazine interviewed some terminally ill patients who had purchased the book. All were alert and lively, and said they would use the suicide information if and when their condition worsened. They made comments like: "*Final Exit* has made me see that I've got a way out. I don't want to be a vegetable"; "I don't have to worry about friends collecting money to pay the hospital. My death is going to be calm and pleasant and even beautiful"; and "I've always had control over my life. I just want to have control over my own death."[6]

But while it was intended for the terminally ill, *Final Exit* was sold at popular bookstores and could be purchased by anyone. For this reason the book was widely criticized by people who felt the information it provided could easily be misused.

Even Dr. Timothy E. Quill, who referred a patient with leukemia to the Hemlock Society and used the group's suggestions to assist her in committing suicide (the case is discussed in the next chapter), found reason for concern. He was troubled that people following *Final Exit*'s instructions would not receive proper professional counseling. "There is no control over who gets the information and whether it is used under the right conditions," he said.[7]

Above all, critics feared that people who were emotionally disturbed might use the information to commit suicide. Robert Boorstin, the co-leader of a mood disorder support group, pointed out in a *New York Times* op-ed piece that three out of every four suicides are committed by people with depression. He said that clinical depression is caused by a chemical imbalance in the brain and is treatable through medication, hospitalization, therapy, and support. The problem with *Final Exit*, he believes, is that while depressed people do not need to kill themselves, the book makes it easier to do so:

> I have known and talked to people who have thought a lot about suicide, who mention it often, but are too scared to try. They are afraid that they will fail in their attempt, that, as one told me recently, "it might not work." Thanks to Derek Humphry's book, that's one worry they can cross off their lists.[8]

Other critics, opposed to assisted suicide as both illegal and unethical, criticized the book for providing "how-to" suicide information to doctors. Dr. Lonnie R. Bristow, an internist in San Pablo, California, who is on the board of the American Medical Association, called this "repugnant" and said, "It strikes at the very foundation of what makes the [medical] profession noble." He added that there was "no reason in this day and age for a patient to have unbearable suffering" and that trust in doctors would be undermined "if there is reason to believe that doctors are equally adept at killing as well as saving lives."[9]

However much some people disapproved of the book, though, there was little they could do about it. First Amendment free-speech guarantees mean that any book, no matter what its content, can be produced and distributed, and most bookstores were willing to carry *Final Exit.* The book had found a huge audience, and none of the criticism it received could change that fact.

6

When Doctors
Aid in Suicide

Dr. Kevorkian and His Suicide Machine

Janet Adkins of Portland, Oregon, had "an absolute zest for living," in the words of one of her friends. She was an English teacher, and with her husband she had raised three sons, now all grown. She enjoyed hang gliding, ballooning, trekking in the Himalayas, and she had climbed the highest mountain in Oregon.

Adkins especially loved to play the piano. But one day she found herself forgetting songs she had known all her life. Soon she lost her ability to read music. On June 12, 1989, doctors told her why—though only in her mid-fifties, she was suffering from Alzheimer's disease.

Alzheimer's patients often live for many years after

first being diagnosed, with symptoms worsening gradually. Adkins could still function, but she faced a bleak future. Eventually she would experience severe memory loss and dementia, just as Emily Gilbert had (see Chapter 5). Her loved ones would have to care for her, or she would face life in an institution, at great financial cost to her family. Her pathetic condition would end in her death.

She decided to take control while she still could. She started planning her suicide. She had seen a doctor named Jack Kevorkian on the television program *Donahue*, and she had read about him in *Newsweek* magazine. Kevorkian, a passionate, some say fanatical, right-to-die advocate, had invented, but not yet used, a "suicide machine," a device with which patients could painlessly take their own lives under his supervision. She contacted the doctor.

Jack Kevorkian was a sixty-two-year-old pathologist whose advocacy of euthanasia and other controversial medical practices had made him an outcast from his profession. He had not held a job since 1982, spending his time writing and working on his suicide machine. "My ultimate aim is to make euthanasia a positive experience," he said. "I'm trying to knock the medical profession into accepting its responsibilities, and those responsibilities include assisting their patients with death."[1]

When after six months the experimental treatments

she was taking for her disease proved ineffective, Adkins decided to fly to Michigan. Over dinner at a restaurant near Kevorkian's suburban home, he told her how his machine worked. In his judgment, she was alert and understood. He would take no fee for his efforts.

Motels and funeral homes would not allow Kevorkian to use their premises to carry out his plan. So instead he used his rusting 1968 Volkswagen van, which he outfitted for the occasion with a cot, new curtains, new bed linens—and the suicide device. On June 4, 1990, he drove with Adkins to a local park.

The suicide machine consisted of three bottles of liquids hanging upside down inside a frame. One bottle held a harmless saline solution; the next held thiopental, a barbiturate that causes unconsciousness; and the third contained potassium chloride, a compound that stops the heart. Kevorkian hooked Adkins up to the device using an intravenous tube.

After Kevorkian started the flow of the saline, Adkins pressed a button. An electric-clock motor with a pulley axle sent the barbiturate and then the lethal drug into her body. She died in less than six minutes. According to Kevorkian, just before dying, "she looked at me with grateful eyes and said, 'Thank you, thank you, thank you.'" The doctor then called the police and reported what had happened.

Adkins had written a suicide note hours before going to die. It said:

> I have decided for the following reasons to take my own life. This is a decision taken in a normal state of mind and is fully considered. I have Alzheimer's disease and I do not want to let it progress any further. I do not want to put my family or myself through the agony of this terrible disease.[2]

Doctors and medical ethicists blasted Kevorkian and his suicide device. Even many staunch right-to-die advocates found his actions extreme and unsavory. They criticized the doctor for assisting in the suicide of a person who was basically a stranger to him. They said that as a pathologist he was not in a position to know Adkins's health status or outlook, or whether she was of sufficiently sound mind to rationally make the decision to die. They declared that he had no business taking such a drastic action without consulting other doctors. They accused him of conflict of interest—being eager for a test case to advance his cause.

Medical experts found another problem with Adkins's suicide: She could have had many more years with a reasonably good quality of life. In the week before her death, her symptoms were still mild enough that she could play tennis with her thirty-two-year-old son, and win. Also, Alzheimer's is difficult to diagnose with certainty. (On the other hand, if the diagnosis were correct and she had waited to die, she might have lost her mind before she could have successfully committed suicide.)

Kevorkian, who calls himself an "obitiatrist" (death doctor), acknowledged that the death of Janet Adkins had not taken place in the best possible circumstances. But he argued that this was an inevitable result of the prohibitions against assisted suicide enforced by legal authorities and the medical establishment.

Kevorkian doesn't believe that Adkins should have had to fly halfway across the country to get her wish. Instead, he wants assisted suicide to be widely available and accessible to anyone who needs it. Ideally, he says, it would not be performed by physicians but by salaried nonmedical workers in special nonprofit suicide clinics he calls "obitoriums."

County prosecutors did not share this vision, and they charged Kevorkian with first-degree murder. Kevorkian said he had not committed murder because Adkins had given herself the lethal dose of drugs. The coroner's office agreed, calling Adkins's death a suicide; a judge then dismissed the murder charges against the doctor, noting that Michigan had no law against assisted suicide. But a civil court issued an injunction barring him from using the suicide machine again.

Kevorkian insisted that the service he provided was not against state law, and he promised to defy the judge's ban. On October 23, 1991, he kept his promise, carrying out a double assisted suicide in a cabin in another Michigan park. Two Michigan women—Sherry Miller, forty-three, who had multiple sclerosis, and Marjorie Wantz, fifty-eight, who suffered from a painful pelvic disease—were attached to two new suicide devices and died within an hour of each other. Neither was a patient of Kevorkian's and neither was terminally ill.

Both women had pleaded with the doctor for two years to help them commit suicide. They expressed a desire to die right after the sun went down, on a warm day. When Kevorkian finally decided to grant their wish, he took them to the cabin together, fearing that if he helped only one, he would be stopped by the police before he could assist the other.

Again, Kevorkian's actions were greeted with outrage. Michigan state senator Fred Dillingham, who had introduced legislation to make assisting a suicide a felony, said:

> We're looking at somebody who wants to be Dr. God. It's a very scary concept. He violated a court order, violated medical ethics, then turns around and broadens [the category of people he'll help to die] to the chronically ill. It makes me wonder what's next if we don't get him checked in this state.[3]

A medical examiner judged the deaths to be murder. Although Kevorkian was indicted by a grand jury, again a judge dismissed first-degree murder charges against him. By December 1992 Kevorkian had helped another five gravely ill women to kill themselves. The Michigan legislature responded by passing a law banning assisted suicide in the state for fifteen months. In the meantime, a panel of experts would study the issue and make recommendations on whether or not the practice should be legal. Penalties for violating the law included a sentence of up to four years in prison and a $2,000 fine. Before the legislation took effect, Kevorkian assisted several more suicides. He said he would ignore the law, calling it "irrelevant to me."

Dr. Timothy Quill and Diane: A Model for Assisted Suicide?

It seemed so unfair. Diane, forty-five, had had such a difficult life—contracting vaginal cancer as a young woman; suffering, for much of her adulthood, from loneliness, depression, and alcoholism.[4] For the past three and a half years, though, she had been turning her life around. She had given up drinking, deepened family relationships and friendships, made advances in her work, and acquired a new self-confidence. As Timothy Quill, her doctor of eight years, told the story, she was just beginning to live fully. But then Quill, an internist at Genesee Hospital in Rochester, New York, diagnosed her with leukemia—blood cancer. On hearing the bad news, Quill wrote, "she was terrified, angry, and sad."

He told her that with treatment—a course of

chemotherapy followed by a bone marrow transplant—she had a one-in-four chance of survival; without it she would surely die in weeks or months. Diane had seen relatives and friends go through chemotherapy, and she believed their deaths had been very unpleasant. According to Quill, "She was convinced she would die during a period of treatment and would suffer unspeakably in the process—from hospitalization, from lack of control over her body, from the side effects of chemotherapy, and from pain and anguish." She decided against treatment, saying she preferred to go home and be with her husband and college-age son.

Diane discussed her decision with a psychologist who had previously counseled her. She also spoke many times with Quill, who made sure she had a clear understanding of her options. Although at first he was disturbed by her refusal to be treated, he eventually came to understand Diane's point of view and see that "it was the right decision for her." He arranged for her to have home hospice care.

In the course of their discussions, Diane raised a new concern—although she was still feeling well enough and was active, when her condition deteriorated, she wanted to end her life painlessly by committing suicide. "It was extremely important to Diane to maintain control of herself and her own dignity," Quill wrote. Quill, who had directed a hospice program, knew how to use painkillers to keep patients comfortable until they died, but Diane did not want to linger this way. She discussed this with her family, who believed they should respect her choice.

Quill said he felt "uneasy" about helping Diane die, an act that had profound legal and moral implications. But he was a staunch advocate of patient self-determination, and he reasoned that Diane would be happier in the time remaining to her, and better able to focus on the present, if she knew she could control her death when the time came. He also worried that if he did not provide her with a way to do this, a family member would have to. Or, she might try suicide unsuccessfully and be left in a horrible condition. He decided to put her in touch with the Hemlock Society.

Later, at Diane's request, Quill wrote her a prescription for barbiturates, after making sure she was not suffering from a temporary depression. Although she needed them to help her sleep, the two also discussed what the pills would ultimately be used for. Quill told her how many to take to commit suicide.

Diane got a lot out of the time she had left. She had intimate discussions with family and friends. She visited the hospital to discuss with physicians the issue of patient decision-making and treatment refusal. But, wrote Quill:

> Unfortunately, we had no miracle. Bone pain, weakness, fatigue, and fevers began to dominate her life. Although the hospice workers, family

members, and I tried our best to minimize the suffering and promote comfort, it was clear that the end was approaching. Diane's immediate future held what she feared the most—increasing discomfort, dependence, and hard choices between pain and sedation.

Diane said goodbye to her friends and her doctor. Two days later she said her last words to her husband and son, and asked them to leave her alone for an hour. Then she took the barbiturates.

Quill, called in by the family, reported the death to officials as having been caused by acute leukemia, without mentioning the pills. He wanted to protect himself and Diane's family from legal prosecution.

In March 1991 Quill told the story of Diane's death in *The New England Journal of Medicine*. Now he was taking a small chance that he would be legally prosecuted. (In New York it's a crime to "intentionally cause or aid another person to commit suicide"; violations carry a five- to fifteen-year prison sentence.) Quill also risked being disciplined by a medical review board. Despite this, he wanted to advance the debate over assisted suicide by presenting a case that answered many of the ethical objections raised by the practices of Jack Kevorkian.

As it turned out, a grand jury refused to indict Quill. The Board for Professional Medical Conduct, while not condoning assisted suicide, ruled his actions were "legal and ethically appropriate" because "he could not know with certainty what use a patient might make of the drugs he had prescribed."[5]

Many medical ethicists found Quill's actions morally acceptable and possibly a model for how doctor-assisted suicide should be performed. Unlike Kevorkian, Quill had a long-established relationship with his patient and provided her with good care. He knew Diane to be mentally competent, and her family supported her decision. He said he could never do what Kevorkian had done. "The difference in the cases is like night and day," said George Annas, a health policy lawyer at Boston University.[6]

Some doctors said that physician-assisted suicide was a common practice, but a rarely discussed one, and they were glad Quill had brought it into the open. One ethicist said that more than twelve physicians had told him in secret that they had assisted in the suicides of their patients. Two had given patients lethal injections.[7]

The *New York Times* editorialized that doctors should be allowed to assist in suicides "if they do it as carefully as Dr. Quill did." Laws against assisted suicide "deprive patients who rationally choose suicide of the knowledge they need to avoid unimaginable suffering."[8]

But other observers, who focused on the economics of assisted suicide, were less impressed. Syndicated newspaper columnist Julianne Malveaux pointed out that having a doctor like Timothy Quill is a luxury many people cannot afford.[9] Thirty-seven million Americans go without health insurance, and many people who belong to health maintenance organizations don't have a personal physician. For these people the debate over assisted suicide is largely irrelevant, she noted.

And Rita L. Marker, director of the International Anti-Euthanasia Task Force at the University of Steubenville, in Ohio, worried that poor people would suffer if assisted suicide were legalized.[10] If they became seriously ill and an economic burden on family and society, they would be encouraged to kill themselves. She said that economics "will make assisted suicide an 'option' for the rich, but it may well become the only affordable 'treatment' for the poor," and that people who approved of Quill's actions were "looking at the salesman and not the product."

Marker also said of Quill, "I think he very clearly assisted her and nudged her toward taking her own life. I believe that is a crime and should be a crime."[11]

7

Should Active Euthanasia Be Legalized?

Active Euthanasia in the Netherlands

Active euthanasia and assisted suicide are performed more widely and openly in the Netherlands than anywhere else in the world. Because of this, for both euthanasia opponents and advocates in the United States, Holland has become a testing ground: Can a policy allowing this practice succeed or is it destined to fail? Although euthanasia is technically illegal in the Netherlands, Dutch courts and the Parliament have drawn up guidelines under which doctors, and doctors alone, may end a patient's life without facing criminal prosecution. These guidelines are listed below.

- The patient must repeatedly and explicitly ask to die.

- The patient must have full information, and the decision to die must be voluntary and enduring.

- The patient must be experiencing unbearable suffering.

- All alternatives acceptable to the patient for relieving the suffering have been tried.

- The patient's doctor must consult with at least one other doctor whose judgment can be expected to be independent.

- The physician must tell public officials that euthanasia has taken place.

Patients who ask for euthanasia in the Netherlands are most likely to be cancer patients in their early sixties who fear loss of dignity, pain, and dependence. In most cases the euthanasia is carried out by the family doctor in the patient's home. Usually, he or she gives an injection of a large dose of barbiturates, which produces unconsciousness, followed by a shot of curare, which stops the breathing and the heart. In assisted suicide, the doctor makes a large dose of barbiturates available to the patient, to be taken orally.

A major study commissioned by the Dutch government and published in 1991 looked at the practice of euthanasia.[1] Researchers interviewed doctors, conducted surveys, and examined death certificates.

They found that:

- 2,300 deaths per year, or 1.8 percent of all deaths in the Netherlands, were the result of voluntary euthanasia performed by doctors, and about 400 deaths per year were the result of assisted suicide.

- 57 percent of patients gave loss of dignity as one of the reasons they were requesting death; 46 percent listed pain; 46 percent, "unworthy dying"; 33 percent, dependence on other people; and 23 percent, being tired of life. Pain was listed as the sole reason in less than 6 percent of cases.

- 68 percent of patients who died by euthanasia suffered from cancer, 9 percent from heart disease, 6 percent from lung disease, 2 percent from nervous system diseases, and 15 percent from other conditions.

- In 70 percent of euthanasia deaths the patient's life was shortened by at least one week; in 8 percent it was shortened by more than six months.

- Every year more than 25,000 patients in the Netherlands ask their doctor for assurance that he or she would be willing to resort to euthanasia if their suffering became unbearable; about one-third of these patients go on to seriously request euthanasia. Doctors turn down about two-thirds of serious euthanasia requests, providing alternative care instead.

Both opponents and supporters of euthanasia have

used the study to buttress their position. Deborah Senn, a Seattle lawyer and pro-euthanasia activist, said the study showed that the practice of euthanasia was "self-limiting" and "really rebuts the argument" that euthanasia is "out of control in the Netherlands."[2]

Euthanasia supporters also could point to the fact that many of the doctors who had performed euthanasia said they would be reluctant to do it again and would do so only if their patient was suffering greatly and there were no alternatives. Many doctors "mentioned that an emotional bond is required for euthanasia," according to the Dutch study. The study authors believe that "this may be one reason why euthanasia was more common in general practice, where doctor and patient have often known each other for years and the doctor has shared part of the patient's suffering."

The authors also conclude that doctors' reluctance to practice euthanasia "refutes the 'slippery slope' argument," which says that the practice of euthanasia will lead to greater and greater abuses.

On the other hand, euthanasia opponents cited some statistics suggesting that abuses did indeed occur. For instance, the Dutch study found that every year 1,000 people were put to death even though they had not made explicit and repeated requests for euthanasia. The study authors say that "these patients were close to death and suffering grievously," and that more than half of them had in the past expressed a wish to be helped to die should they experience unbearable suffering, but they had since become mentally incompetent and unable to ask for euthanasia.

To critics, though, the crucial fact was that 1,000 people per year were being killed without their consent—the doctors were violating Dutch legal guidelines and committing *non*voluntary euthanasia. S. G. Potts of the Royal Edinburgh Hospital in Scotland saw it this way: "This is strong evidence that in practice the [legal guidelines] are already being informally extended, precisely as predicted by the slippery slope argument, and in a way that leaves the doctors involved open to a charge of murder."[3]

In another study, physician and public policy analyst Dr. Carlos E. Gomez interviewed Dutch doctors, nurses, bioethicists, and others to collect information on twenty-six cases of euthanasia in the Netherlands.[4]

The most consistent problem he found was that doctors failed to report cases of euthanasia to public officials, as required by law. In several cases physicians just listed "cardiac arrest" on the death certificate as the cause of death, without saying what caused the cardiac arrest—namely, euthanasia. Pro-euthanasia groups in the Netherlands acknowledge that this occurs, but they believe that it is the result of the peculiar laws governing the practice.

Gomez found several other types of abuse. One physician, who performed euthanasia in patients' homes, neglected to get a second opinion before doing so. When

Gomez pointed out that the guidelines required him to do this, the physician got angry and said, "I know my patients better than anyone else."

Sometimes patients were put to death without their consent. In one case, a fifty-six-year-old man suffered massive internal injuries in an auto accident and was dying. In the hospital emergency room a surgeon asked a physician on the intensive care staff if he should operate. The physician responded, "The heart will stop in some time, but if the family comes sooner, they must wait for this; it is a terrible situation."

The physician then gave the patient an injection of potassium chloride to speed the death. Gomez notes that the doctor acted on his own and didn't even wait for the family to arrive to find out if the patient had filled out a living will or had discussed his feelings about euthanasia. The doctor seemed to justify his decision by saying he wanted to spare the family the pain of watching the patient die.

Based on his findings, Gomez urges that euthanasia not be legalized in the United States, where, he fears, it would be subject to even more abuse.

But philosopher Margaret Battin, of the University of Utah, says that such abuses must be understood in context.[5] Just because a practice is subject to abuse, she argues, does not necessarily mean it should be banned. After all, there have been cases in which nurses have randomly injected patients with lethal drugs and surgeons have intentionally performed harmful operations, but no one is proposing that nursing or surgery be prohibited.

Aside from such extreme examples, more common abuses may also occur when people choose high-risk surgery or choose to forgo life-sustaining treatment (passive euthanasia). Battin doesn't think active euthanasia would be any more abused, and she believes that adding certain safeguards in the United States, such as requiring a psychological evaluation and a short waiting period, would make the practice safe here.

The Campaign in the United States

In November 1991 voters in the state of Washington had a chance to decide whether they wanted to go beyond the Netherlands and become the first place in the world to legalize active euthanasia outright. They cast their ballots for or against a referendum known as Initiative 119, "A Voluntary Choice . . . for Death with Dignity."

If passed, terminally ill adults in the state would be able to ask a doctor to end their lives "in a dignified, painless and humane manner"—by providing lethal drugs, for instance. The measure would override existing Washington law, which made assisted suicide a felony. The initiative also contained a far less controversial provision that allowed the practice of passive euthanasia to be expanded.

A volunteer collecting signatures for Initiative 119 to legalize active euthanasia in the state of Washington. The petition drive gathered 223,000 signatures.

Safeguards were included to prevent abuse of active euthanasia: the patient would have to be mentally competent; two doctors would have to agree that the patient had less than six months to live; and the patient would be required to ask for euthanasia in writing, in front of two unrelated witnesses.

Of the people discussed in this book, most would not have been allowed to receive active euthanasia under the Washington initiative: Karen Quinlan and Nancy Cruzan because they were unconscious and couldn't ask for it; quadriplegic Larry McAfee because he was not terminally ill, just disabled; Emily Gilbert and Janet Adkins because they were not in the final stages of Alzheimer's. Ida Rollins and "Diane," however, with their late-stage cancers, probably would have been able to ask for a doctor's help in dying.

Supporters and opponents of Initiative 119 fought an expensive and heated campaign. Advocates included the Hemlock Society of Washington State, the state Democratic party, gay rights groups, and groups supporting rights for the elderly. Among the opponents were right-to-life organizations and the Catholic Church in Washington, medical groups, and the state Republican party.

Urging people to vote "no," foes of 119 appealed to basic principles forbidding killing. University of Michigan law professor Yale Kamisar cited eminent bioethicist Tom Beauchamp to explain his opposition: "Rules against killing, [Beauchamp] pointed out, are not isolated moral principles but pieces of a web that forms a moral code. 'The more threads one removes,' Mr. Beauchamp warned, 'the weaker the fabric becomes.' "[6]

The initiative's backers also appealed to an overriding principle: self-determination. Susan Baron of Seattle, who lost a leg to bone cancer, an extremely painful disease, said it should be her business alone if she chooses to die. A former antique shop owner, Baron said, "The medicine doesn't take away the pain. It's still there, and it's excruciating. Most of us don't die painful deaths, but those of us that do shouldn't have to."[7]

Opponents were also concerned about the effects the legislation could have on the way people saw doctors and doctoring. A statement drafted by three bishops said, "Asking doctors to kill undermines the moral integrity and confidence in a profession that heals, comforts and protects life."[8]

Opponents feared a variety of abuses that they believed could result from legalizing euthanasia: The poor, the elderly, the disabled, and the uninsured would be pressured to choose euthanasia if their health care became too costly; voluntary euthanasia would lead to involuntary euthanasia. They used the Netherlands as an example, saying that studies (see above) showed that euthanasia was abused there.

They could also point to differences between the United States and the Netherlands that might make euthanasia more problematic here. Teresa A. Takken, an

The Reverend Ralph Mero, president of the Washington State chapter of the Hemlock Society, was an author of the Washington ballot initiative on euthanasia.

ethicist at the Goleta Valley Hospital in Santa Barbara, California, believes that the practice of euthanasia would be much more subject to abuse in the United States, where poverty is more widespread than it is in Holland, with its generous health care and welfare programs. "We have no business even talking about euthanasia here," she said, "until we have health care for all, and even housing for all."[9]

But Initiative 119 advocate James Vorenberg, who teaches criminal law at Harvard Law School, argued that greater risks of abuse from euthanasia arise from its illegality.[10] He said that some physicians already practice euthanasia, and prosecutors rarely investigate the cause of death. When euthanasia is practiced illegally, patients are at risk because there are no safeguards to protect their rights. The doctor has too much power.

Patients would receive greater protection under the proposed Washington law, according to Vorenberg, because it would provide safeguards ensuring that the patient is mentally competent and acting voluntarily. "For those terrified of ending their lives in pain and degradation that they lack the ability to end, and for those who worry about the Kevorkians who may be too willing and ready to provide assistance, the carefully limited and protective procedures of the Washington initiative offer promise," Vorenberg said.

Vorenberg also dismissed opponents' fears of a "slippery slope" scenario in which legalizing voluntary euthanasia would lead to other kinds of allowed killings. He pointed out that exceptions are already made to prohibitions against killing—such as capital punishment and killing in self-defense—without this consequence.

Until close to Election Day, it seemed that Initiative 119 would win easily. A nationwide poll conducted during the campaign showed 64 percent of Americans were in favor of allowing doctors to give lethal medications to incurably sick patients. But, ultimately, in Washington, enough voters had doubts that the measure was defeated by a small margin, 54–46%.

According to a *New York Times* editorial, voters rejecting 119 were most concerned about two issues: that people would choose euthanasia so as not to become a burden on their family, and that patients misdiagnosed as being terminally ill would elect to die even though their lives might have been longer.[11]

After the loss in Washington, pro-euthanasia forces succeeded in placing a similar initiative on the California ballot for November 1992. Several safeguards not contained in the Washington measure were added to address voter concerns over the potential for abuses: a nursing-home patient's written request for euthanasia must be signed in the presence of a patient's rights advocate and one other person unrelated to the patient; a doctor could request a psychological consultation for the patient to make sure he is mentally competent; a patient must ask his doctor for euthanasia at least two times; and doctors must make a report to state health authorities when they have performed euthanasia. But voter worries were not alleviated, and this initiative failed as well, by the same margin as the Washington measure.

Passive euthanasia, although not a settled issue, is a subject about which U.S. citizens have reached something of a consensus. It is widely agreed that people should be able to refuse medical care even if this will result in their death; that close family members of an unconscious patient should have the right to order the withdrawal of life-preserving treatment from the patient in accordance with the patient's wishes; and that advance directives, although not perfect, are a good idea. But the debate in the United States on active euthanasia is at a much earlier stage.

Some people say that, as abortion was the social issue of the 1980s in the United States, euthanasia will be the social issue of the 1990s. How it will finally be resolved no one can predict. Will it divide the country as the abortion debate has? Or will we be able to reach a consensus on active euthanasia as we have on passive euthanasia? If active euthanasia is legalized, will the safeguards work? Or will the grim predictions made by its opponents come true? One thing can be predicted though: the debate over euthanasia will remain complex and highly emotional, and the result will touch everyone's life . . . and many people's deaths.

Chapter Notes

*All *New York Times* references cite the local edition unless "national ed." is noted.

Chapter 2

1. Information and quotes on the Quinlan case come from the following sources:

> Phyllis Battelle, " 'Let Me Sleep': The Story of Karen Ann Quinlan," *Ladies Home Journal,* September 1976, pp. 69–76+.

> B. D. Colen, "The Long Dying of Karen Ann Quinlan," *McCall's,* September 1976, pp. 50, 55–56+.

> "Karen's Precedent," *Time,* April 12, 1976, p. 50.

> C. Everett Koop, *The Right to Live, The Right to Die* (Wheaton, Ill.: Tyndale, 1976), pp. 102–111, in Robert M. Baird and Stuart E. Rosenbaum (eds.), *Euthanasia: The Moral Issues* (Buffalo, N.Y.: Prometheus, 1989), pp. 35–43.

> "Life in the Balance," *Time,* November 3, 1975, pp. 57–58, 61.

2. Personal correspondence with Bruce Jennings, executive director of the Hastings Center, August 24, 1992.

3. Phyllis Battelle, " 'Let Me Sleep': The Story of Karen Ann Quinlan," *Ladies Home Journal,* September 1976, p. 71.

4. Except where otherwise indicated, information and quotes on the Cruzan case come from the following sources:

> "Anger in Hospital at a Death Order," *New York Times,* December 16, 1990, p. 29.

> "Bringing an End to Limbo," *Time,* December 24, 1990, p. 64.

> Choice in Dying, Fact Sheet on Cruzan case, 1990.

> Deborah Beroset Diamond, "Private Agony, Public Cause," *Ladies Home Journal,* June 1990, pp. 125, 178–182.

Linda Greenhouse, "Justices Find a Right to Die," *New York Times*, June 26, 1990, pp. A1, A19.

Nat Hentoff, "The Judge Who Would Not Kill," *The Village Voice*, June 13, 1989, p. 20.

Nat Hentoff, "Would You Kill Nancy Cruzan?" *The Village Voice*, June 6, 1989, p. 19.

"Nancy Cruzan," *People Weekly*, Dec. 31, 1990–Jan. 7, 1991, p. 59.

David Oliver Relin, "Between Life and Death," *Scholastic Update* (teachers' ed.), January 26, 1990, pp. 20–22.

5. *Missouri* v. *Cruzan*, reprinted in Robert M. Baird and Stuart E. Rosenbaum (eds.), *Euthanasia: The Moral Issues* (Buffalo, N.Y.: Prometheus, 1989), pp. 207–208.

6. *Missouri* v. *Cruzan,* in Baird and Rosenbaum, p. 208.

7. "Right to Die: The Public's View," *New York Times*, June 26, 1990, p. A18.

8. Peter Steinfels, "Bishops Warn on Stopping Life Supports for Comatose," *New York Times*, April 3, 1992, p. A10.

9. Both quotes in this paragraph are from Gina Kolata, "Ethicists Debate New Definition of Death," *New York Times*, April 29, 1992, p. C13.

10. Margot L. White and John C. Fletcher, "The Patient Self-Determination Act," *Journal of the American Medical Association,* July 17, 1991, p. 411.

11. Helene M. Cole, "Advance Directives on Admission," *Journal of the American Medical Association,* July 17, 1991, p. 404.

Other sources for "One Solution: The Advance Directive":

Lisa Belkin, "A Ticklish New Job for Hospitals: Querying Patients on Death Plans," *New York Times*, December 1, 1991, pp. 1, 30.

Andrew Purvis, "When Patients Call the Shots," *Time*, December 9, 1991, p. 75.

Chapter 3

1. Except where otherwise indicated, information and quotes on the treatment of critically ill infants are from the following sources:

Nat Hentoff, "Is It Discriminatory to Kill Handicapped Infants?" *The Village Voice*, March 11, 1986, p. 32.

Gina Kolata, "Parents of Tiny Infants Find Care Choices Are Not Theirs," *New York Times*, September 30, 1991, pp. A1, A14.

Mildred Stahlman, "Implications of Research and High Technology for Neonatal Intensive Care," *Journal of the American Medical Association*, March 24/31, 1989, p. 1791.

Dick Thompson, "Should Every Baby Be Saved?" *Time*, June 11, 1990, pp. 81–82.

2. Howard French, "Tiny Miracles Become Huge Public Health Problem," *New York Times*, February 19, 1989, p. 44.

3. "Life in the Balance," *Time*, November 3, 1975, p. 57.

4. Except where otherwise noted, information and quotes on the case of Larry McAfee come from the following sources:

Peter Applebome, "An Angry Man Fights to Die, Then Tests Life," *New York Times*, February 7, 1990, pp. A1, A21.

Peter Applebome, "Judge Rules Quadriplegic Can Be Allowed to End Life," *New York Times*, September 7, 1989, p. A16 (A12, national ed.).

"Invalid Allowed to Remove Device," *New York Times*, November 22, 1989, p. A18.

Nat Hentoff, "Helping Larry James McAfee Die," *Washington Post*, October 7, 1989, p. A23.

5. Quotes in this paragraph and the previous one are from Paul K. Longmore, "The Shameful Treatment of Larry McAfee," *Atlanta Journal-Constitution,* September 10, 1989, pp. B1, B3.

6. Derek Humphry, *Final Exit: Self-Deliverance and Assisted Suicide for the Dying* (Eugene, Ore.: Hemlock Society, 1991), pp. 58–59.

Chapter 5

1. Information and quotes on the story of Betty and Ida Rollin come from the following sources:

"8 Years Later, Rollin Has No Regrets," *Daily News,* July 21, 1991, p. 26.

Betty Rollin, "My Mother's Last Wish" (excerpt from *Last Wish*), *Good Housekeeping,* October 1985, pp. 127, 246–256.

Betty Rollin, "One Last Wish," *Family Circle,* November 6, 1990, p. 170.

Karen S. Schneider and Sue Carswell, "Love Unto Death," *People,* January 20, 1992, pp. 56, 58–60, 63.

2. Information and quotes on the Roswell Gilbert case come from the following sources:

"The Agony Did Not End for Roswell Gilbert, Who Killed His Wife to Give Her Peace," *People,* January 12, 1987, pp. 31, 32, 35.

Mike Clary, "'Mercy Killing' Inmate Going Free," *Los Angeles Times,* August 2, 1990, p. A28.

Pat Jordan, "Murderer or Model Husband?" *50 Plus,* August 1988, pp. 24–25, 76+.

"Merciless Jury," *Time,* May 27, 1985, pp. 66–67.

Berkeley Rice, "Was It Compassion . . . or Cold Blood?" *50 Plus,* September 1986, pp. 28–30, 32+.

"Roswell Gilbert: The Verdict Is In," *50 Plus*, November 1986, pp. 76–79.

3. Derek Humphry, *Final Exit: Self-Deliverance and Assisted Suicide for the Dying* (Eugene, Ore.: Hemlock Society, 1991), p. 19.

4. Quoted in Lawrence K. Altman, "How-To Book on Suicide Is Atop Best-Seller List," *New York Times*, August 9, 1991, p. A10 (A1, national ed.).

5. Anna Quindlen, "Death: The Best Seller," *New York Times*, August 14, 1991, p. A19.

6. Michelle Green, "The Last Goodbye," *People Weekly*, November 25, 1991, pp. 125–126, 128, 130.

7. Quoted in Altman, p. A10.

8. Robert O. Boorstin, "When Suicide Is Not a Choice," *New York Times*, August 22, 1991, p. A27 (A23, national ed.).

9. Quoted in Altman, p. A10.

Chapter 6

1. Lisa Belkin, "Doctor Tells of First Death Using His Suicide Device," *New York Times*, June 6, 1990, p. A1.

2. Belkin, p. A1.

3. Isabel Wilkerson, "Opponents Weigh Action Against Doctor Who Aided Suicides," *New York Times*, October 25, 1991, p. A10 (A1, national ed.).

4. Diane's story is told in Timothy E. Quill, "Death and Dignity: A Case of Individualized Decision Making," *The New England Journal of Medicine*, March 7, 1991, pp. 691–94.

5. "Doctor Who Aided Suicide Cleared of Misconduct," *Los Angeles Times*, August 18, 1991.

6. Quoted in Lawrence K. Altman, "Doctor Says He Agonized, but Gave Drug for Suicide," *New York Times*, March 7, 1991, p. A12.

105

7. Lawrence K. Altman, "More Physicians Broach Forbidden Subject of Euthanasia," *New York Times*, March 12, 1991, p. C3.

8. "Dealing Death or Mercy?" *New York Times*, March 17, 1991, section 4, p. E16.

9. Julianne Malveaux, "For Millions, This Isn't the Issue," *USA Today*, March 12, 1991, p. 8A.

10. Rita Marker, "Don't Open the Door to Assisted Suicide," *USA Today*, March 12, 1991, p. 8A.

11. Quoted in William Glaberson, "Panel to Decide: Should Doctor Who Aided Suicide Be Tried?" *New York Times*, July 22, 1991, p. B2.

Other sources for "Jack Kevorkian and His Suicide Machine":

Marcia Angell, "Don't Criticize Doctor Death . . . " *New York Times*, June 14, 1990, p. A27.

Natalie Angier, "Diagnosis of Alzheimer's Is No Matter of Certainty," *New York Times*, June 7, 1990, p. D22.

Ron Rosenbaum, "Angel of Death," *Vanity Fair*, May 1991, pp. 147–151, 203–211.

"Doctor Faces Murder Trial for Suicide Aid," *New York Times*, February 29, 1992, p. 10.

Timothy Egan, "As Memory and Music Faded, Oregon Woman Chose Death," *New York Times*, June 7, 1990, pp. A1, D22.

Isabel Wilkerson, "Physician Fulfills a Goal: Aiding a Person in Suicide," *New York Times*, June 7, 1990, p. D22.

Chapter 7

1. The study was summarized in Paul J. van der Maas, et al., "Euthanasia and Other Medical Decisions Concerning the End of Life," *The Lancet*, September 14, 1991, pp. 669–74.

2. Quoted in Peter Steinfels, "Dutch Study Is Euthanasia Vote Issue," *New York Times*, November 2, 1991, p. 11 (10, national ed.).

3. S. G. Potts, "Euthanasia and Other Medical Decisions About the End of Life" (letter), *The Lancet*, October 12, 1991, p. 952.

4. Carlos F. Gomez, *Regulating Death: Euthanasia and the Case of the Netherlands* (New York: The Free Press, 1991).

5. Margaret P. Battin, "Voluntary Euthanasia and the Risks of Abuse: Can We Learn Anything from the Netherlands?" *Law, Medicine & Health Care*, in press.

6. Yale Kamisar, "An Unraveling of Morality," *New York Times*, November 5, 1991, p. A25.

7. Quoted in Joseph P. Shapiro, "A Vote on Legal Euthanasia," *U.S. News & World Report*, September 30, 1991, p. 32.

8. Quoted in Timothy Egan, "Euthanasia Bid in Washington State," *New York Times*, July 6, 1990, p. A9.

9. Quoted in John Horgan, "Death with Dignity," *Scientific American*, March 1991, p. 18.

10. James Vorenberg, "Going Gently, with Dignity," *New York Times*, November 5, 1991, p. A25.

11. "The Voters' Anguish over Death," *New York Times*, November 9, 1991, p. 22 (14, national ed.).

Other source for "Active Euthanasia in the Netherlands":

Marlise Simons, "Dutch Survey Casts New Light on Patients Who Choose to Die," *New York Times*, September 11, 1991, p. B8, national ed.

For Further Information

American Medical Association
515 North State St.
Chicago, IL 60610

Medical Ethics Institutes

The Hastings Center
255 Elm Road
Briarcliff Manor, NY 10510

Joseph and Rose Kennedy Institute of Ethics
1437 37th St., NW
Washington, DC 20057

Advocacy Groups

American Civil Liberties Union
132 W. 43rd St.
New York, NY 10036

Choice in Dying, Inc.
200 Varick St.
10th Floor
New York, NY 10014

Hemlock Society
P.O. Box 11830
Eugene, OR 97440-3900

International Anti-Euthanasia Task Force
The Human Life Center
University of Steubenville
Steubenville, OH 43952

National Conference of Catholic Bishops
Secretariat for Pro-Life Activities
3211 Fourth St., NE
Washington, DC 20017-1194

National Right to Life
Suite 500
419 Seventh St., NW
Washington, DC 20004-2293

Index

A

active euthanasia, 51–59, 64–69,
  87–100. *See also* specific cases.
  abuses of, 56–57, 90–92, 96, 98
  case against legalizing, 56–59
  case for legalizing, 53–56
  definition of, 13, 51
  laws governing, 51, 68
  methods of carrying out, 88
Adkins, Janet, 75–79
advance directives, 27, 30, 31–38,
  100
  problems with, 36, 38
  and sanctity-of-life perspective,
    38
AIDS, 50
Alzheimer's disease, 50, 51, 65–66,
  75–76, 78
American Civil Liberties Union, 12
American Medical Association, 12,
  52
Americans United for Life, 68
Anderson, Jan, 42
anencephaly, 31
artificial nutrition and hydration.
  See feeding by tube.
assisted suicide, 51–64, 69–100.
  See also active euthanasia;
  specific cases.
  definition of, 13, 51
  laws governing, 51, 79, 84
  methods of carrying out, 63,
    69, 71, 83, 88
Association for Retarded Citizens,
  12

B

Baron, Susan, 96

Battelle, Phyllis, 15, 17
Battin, Margaret, 92–93
Boorstin, Robert, 73–74
brain death, 16, 31

C

California euthanasia referendum,
  99–100
cancer, 50, 60, 62, 81
Caplan, Arthur, 71
Catholic Church, 17, 18, 30, 95
chemotherapy, 60, 62, 82
Choice in Dying, 12, 33, 46
Congress, 33
court cases.
  Cruzan, Nancy, 25–29
  Gilbert, Roswell, 67
  McAfee, Larry James, 44–46
  Quinlan, Karen Ann, 18–20
Cranford, Ronald, 31
Cruzan, Christy, 22
Cruzan, Joe, 22, 24, 25, 29
Cruzan, Joyce, 22, 25
Cruzan, Nancy, 21–30
  and abuses of passive
    euthanasia, 26
  evidence of wishes, 22, 24, 26,
    27, 28
  expense of care for, 22
  and persistent vegetative state,
    21, 25, 28
  quality of life, 26
  removal of feeding tube from,
    24, 26, 28
  use of feeding tube for, 21, 22

D

death. *See also* brain death.
  control over, 55, 73, 83

definition of 16, 30–31
with dignity, 71, 82, 93
Declaration of Independence, 28
depression, 53, 57–58, 73–74
Dillingham, Fred, 80
disabled people, discrimination against, 41, 46–47
doctor-patient relationship, 58–59, 96
doctors' mistakes, 11–12

E
euthanasia. *See also* active euthanasia; passive euthanasia.
definition of, 12–13

F
feeding by tube, 21, 22, 24, 25, 27
removal of, 24, 26, 28, 46
Final Exit (suicide manual), 47, 64, 69–74
criticism of, 73
use of, 72–73
Fletcher, John, 31
French, Howard W., 40

G
Gilbert, Emily, 64–68
Gilbert, Roswell, 64–69
convicted of murder, 67
Gomez, Carlos E., 91–92
Grant, Edward R., 68

H
Haig, James, 47
health care *See* medical care.
health care proxy, 33, 38. *See also* advance directives.
Hemlock Society, 52, 69, 73, 83, 95
Hippocratic oath, 52
hospice care, 55, 58, 82, 83
Humphry, Derek, 47, 69–71, 74

I
illness, terminal, 7, 8, 69, 72. *See also* cancer.
infants, critically ill, 39–43
aggressive treatment of, 42
withholding treatment from, 41
infants, intensive care for, 40
infants, premature, 39–40
Initiative 119. *See* Washington euthanasia referendum.
International Anti-Euthanasia Task Force, 12

K
Kamisar, Yale, 95
Kevorkian, Jack, 76–81
charged with murder, 79
criticism of, 78
killing, moral opposition to, 56, 95–96
"killing" vs. "letting die," 9, 10, 52

L
Last Wish, 61, 64
living will, 33. *See also* advance directives.
Longmore, Paul K., 46

M
Marker, Rita L., 86
Martinez, Bob, 69
McAfee, Larry James, 43–47
medical care, expense of,
and passive euthanasia, 11, 22, 43, 47
and assisted suicide & active euthanasia, 51, 57, 76, 86, 98
medical technology, advances in, 7, 8, 40
and prolongation of life, 8, 31, 33, 50–51
mercy killing. *See* active euthanasia.
Mero, Ralph, 97

Michigan, law banning assisted
    suicide in, 81
Miller, Sherry, 80
Missouri, pro-life law, 26
Missouri, Supreme Court of, 26
Muir, Robert, Jr., 19, 20
Myers, Nancy, 29

N

National Right to Life Committee,
    12, 29
Netherlands, practice of active
    euthanasia in, 55–56, 87–93
    criticism of, 90–92
    defense of, 90, 92–93
    legal guidelines governing,
        55–56, 87–88
    and patients who request
        euthanasia, 88
    study on, 88–90
New Jersey, Supreme Court of, 20
nursing homes, 66, 72

O

osteoporosis, 66

P

pain and suffering, 54, 55, 58,
    82–84, 96
passive euthanasia, 7–48, 100. *See
    also* specific cases.
    abuses of, 11, 19, 26, 30, 46
    definition of, 8
Patient Self-Determination Act,
    33, 36
patients, unconscious, 7, 8, 14–38.
    See also Cruzan, Nancy.
    and treatment decisions by
        family, 12, 28
    evidence of wishes, 18, 19, 31
persistent vegetative state (PVS), 16
    accuracy of diagnosis, 16
    in Cruzan case, 21, 25, 28
    in Quinlan case, 15, 17, 20
polls.

on active euthanasia, 99
on passive euthanasia, 21, 29–30

Q

quadriplegia, 44, 46, 47
quality of life.
    and active euthanasia, 50–51
    and Adkins case, 78
    and Cruzan case, 26
    and McAfee case, 44, 45
    and Rollin case, 62
    and treatment decisions, 10, 40
Quill, Timothy E., 73, 81–86
    criticism of, 85–86
    praise for, 85
Quindlen, Anna, 72
Quinlan, Joseph, 14, 17, 18, 19
Quinlan, Julia, 14, 18, 20
Quinlan, Karen Ann, 14–15, 17–21
    and abuses of passive
        euthanasia, 19
    disconnection of respirator for,
        17
    evidence of wishes, 18, 19
    right to life, 19
    right to privacy, 18, 20
    use of respirator for, 15

R

Rehnquist, William, 27
religious groups, views on
    euthanasia, 18, 52. *See also*
    Catholic Church.
respirator.
    disconnecting, 9, 17
    in Quinlan case, 15, 18, 20
    in McAfee case, 43–45
right to die, 27, 71
    arguments for, 10, 11
    groups advocating, 12
    groups opposing, 12
right to liberty, 11
right to life, 19
right to privacy, 11, 18, 20, 45

111

right to refuse medical treatment, 20, 27, 44–46
Robertson, Edward, Jr., 26
Rollin, Betty, 60–64
Rollin, Ida, 60–64
Rouse, Fenella, 46

S

sanctity of life.
 and decisions on treatment, 11
 arguments for, 11
self-determination, 53–54, 83, 96
slippery slope argument, 57, 90–91, 98–99
state's interest in life, 11, 28
Stevens, John Paul, 28
suffering. *See* pain and suffering.
suicide, 50, 82
 case of James Haig, 47–48
 machine for carrying out, 76–77
 rational, 53, 55, 57, 64

T

Teel, Charles, Jr., 26, 28, 29
Trapasso, Father Thomas, 17, 18
treatment, extraordinary

feeding by tube as, 25,
 respirator as, 9
 and terminally ill patients, 9
treatment, ordinary, 8
 feeding by tube as, 25, 26
 respirator as, 9–10
treatment, withdrawal of. *See* passive euthanasia.

U

U.S. Constitution, 10, 18, 28
U.S. Supreme Court, 12, 27, 33

V

Vatican, 18
Vorenberg, James, 98–99

W

Wantz, Marjorie, 80
Washington euthanasia referendum, 93–99
 safeguard provisions in, 95, 98
 defeat of, 99